Awakening
Mediu
Third E   ..ıd
Mental Health

A Psychic Medium's
Personal Story
of Questioning Everything
He's Told for the
Sake of His Sanity

Sean Graham

ACKNOWLEDGMENTS

I feel the most relevant thank you, would be to all the clients around the world I have been lucky enough to meet. You trusted me with such a personal experience; some of you even allowing me to share your experiences in this book. You all accepted me for who I was, with my bad language and blunt way with words and I am very grateful. It has been a true honour to be able to share these experiences with every single one of you, and if it wasn't for my amazing clients, I would not have had the drive to write this book. The trust you put in me, means more than I could possibly begin to explain. THANK YOU

The writing of this book has impacted everyone I know personally, none more so than my family. I appreciate you giving me the time and understanding I needed to follow this through.

I would also like to thank the following individuals for all the support, patience, and understanding I have received along the way despite my stubborn, opinionated nature: David Akerman, Konstantina Bellou (Elena the Greek), Ann Macoul, Ronit Sher, Julian Jenkins, Emma Woods and my good friends Chad, Paul, Dave, Andy and Peanut (Ryan) for keeping me grounded in the 'real' world, whilst being accepting of what I was saying.

To everyone above: Some of our views may or may not always be in alignment, but you still gave me support that meant so much to me when I was lost and struggling to work everything out.

A special thank you also to anyone I approached when I was looking for answers or support, who lied to me, misdirected me, or used fear as a tool to sell me something I did not need, or simply to boost your Ego. You highlighted to me the reasons why this book needed to be written and helped me gain the understanding necessary to be able to help my clients. For that I can only be grateful

For You…

This book is for the people I have met who are struggling with emotions and relationships while trying to navigate an awakening, desperate for things to make sense and feeling alone in the world.

You are far from alone...

CONTENTS

SEAN GRAHAM

1.

THINGS NEED TO CHANGE

In no way would I consider myself an author, but I do have points to raise. These are my own words, so I would like to apologise in advance for any bad language used or offence caused. I also ask you to view me and everyone you speak to about anything to do with this subject as "an idiot expressing their views."

Being far from a complete expert on spirituality myself is something that would be expected, and due to the fact that I don't believe we truly can be an expert until we pass, it makes me suspicious of those who do claim to be complete experts, passing on matter-of-fact information with no reasoning other than, "This is how it is."

I have a very cantankerous nature and I believe this was particularly useful to me during my awakening to stop me accepting everything I was told, and instead only accept what I could prove. Using my experiences and what I have witnessed, I hope to help others look at certain things from all sides in a clear light. I have my theories and beliefs, some of them very solid beliefs that have been confirmed to me or proven. The facts I know for sure, because of the evidence I have passed on to clients, is that this life is not all there is.

Loved ones in Spirit have passed me far too much evidence for me to pass to others, to question this, so for that reason I do state that it is a fact that our Spirit lives on. As for all the other stuff that we get bombarded with, let's see what we can make of it all…

This book will hopefully explain my take on a spiritual awakening and why I feel more needs to be done in the understanding of the effect it can have on people. Not just in the 'cult', or what some would call 'crazy' spirituality circles that can, at times, scare off some people, leaving them to cope on their own with no idea of what's happening to them.

An awakening allows us to see life differently, both the good and bad, because we can start to see the world in a clearer light; we can also see the negative a lot clearer too. Unfortunately (or fortunately), that can mean you start to see the bullshit in places you once did not, and that can have a huge impact on you, depending on the circumstance. Although I was never keen on the term "spiritual awakening", it is the term I will use throughout this book to keep things simple.

Personally, getting my head around this whole Spiritual Awakening thing was made even more confusing by the fact that I was trying to believe certain things just because I was told to, as well as a lot of these things also being the views of the masses, making it harder to argue. Sensing Spirit around me and wanting to know what was going on, I naturally looked for answers. The first piece of advice I would give myself, if doing it all over again, would be to take everything as a theory and not let anyone pass their fear on to me.

Question everything unless you are offered evidence or an explanation that makes perfect sense to support what you are told; no matter how many people already believe something, it still needs to be demonstrated to you. Question rules and traditions that make no sense to you because, seriously, who can genuinely say they have all the answers? Every single one and offer no evidence? Questioning everything can save a lot of conflicting information affecting your mental health because trying to accept everything can, for some, be a mental health disaster!

I think it is important to tell my story and talk about my experiences before I talk about how I do this or offer anything "instructional". I use the word instructional very lightly because I can only pass on what works for me; my views, opinions, and what I have seen. It is as simple as that, There are many things I do not understand fully, and would never claim to be an expert.

Not grasping something enough to make sense of it does not necessarily mean that having it explained by someone who does 'understand' automatically make their explanation factual, it makes their explanation a consideration for me to think about until I have proof or an incredibly good explanation. After all, it's no secret that some people just like the sound of their own voice, meaning they use it a lot, regardless of what they are saying. If you shout something enough, even if it's bullshit, you are bound to get some of it to stick. Once some of it sticks, it can be passed on by someone who trusts what they have been told, and some traditions could simply have started this way.

Something must change with how we as humans receive information because there are too many people in mental health turmoil because of conflicting advice. It sometimes even instils fear, without the intention of doing so; I will talk about this later in the book. I have attended countless of readings as a sitter and well over a thousand readings as a reader. I have met some amazing people with unbelievable talents and some of the best mediums and psychics, giving detailed undeniable evidence. Unfortunately, I have also met some people who have told me things that were so dangerous and irresponsible that I have been close to walking away from this industry for fear of being associated with people like that.

As I will explain in detail later, I was once called an irresponsible father for letting my daughter use a candle for divination. This is the daughter who, like my son, has a natural connection with no interference from human teachings and the instilling of fear. My children have no fear of Spirit for that reason; maybe they can teach us something about where fear comes from because they don't seem to have been born with it!

Thanks to readings from, and relationships with, some fantastic lightworkers that I will talk about as we go on, my faith was restored, but this book still needed writing. Even if only one person is helped to live a life with less confusion and anxiety around this subject, it will be worth it.

I am very proud to say that I am still learning and will be for the rest of my life. Through my website, www.seanmedium.com, I carry out mediumship and, at times, psychic readings, sometimes referred to as Remote Viewing readings. While most of them are completely Spirit guided, I do use remote viewing for some aspects, but I feel it is very important to tell my clients how I obtained each piece of information I have passed on. The difference between the two is quite simple, yet particularly important.

Mediumship is simply information from Spirit. In the simplest way of explaining it, the psychic is connecting to your or anyone else's energies and getting information from you, not Spirit. As well as being able to connect psychically, and at the risk of complicating things, I do also personally see everyone as having a Spirit; when we die, the Spirit remains. To simplify, while we are here on Earth, I picture the Spirit as an energy above someone's head or around them, the higher self that we can tap into the same way as if we connect to a Spirit belonging to someone who has passed, except the human that has passed only has the Spirit remaining with continued consciousness.

Evidential-based mediumship has allowed me to pass information to clients and reassure them that loved ones are not gone forever and still here with us. I feel responsible mediumship only offers anything at all if you can first offer evidence to the client—evidence that the person you are talking about can be clearly identified. Sometimes the message itself is that they are here still, and the sceptic in me feels slightly silly pushing for a message just because I need to if one is not forthcoming.

Everyone, I fully believe, has this ability. Some are extremely tuned in but with little understanding of how they are getting messages (this is where we start asking, "Am I crazy?"). I have carried out exercises with hundreds of people to show them the part of their consciousness that is passed off as imagination or, in some cases, just blurred into a fog due to day-to-day human life stresses and noise. What I am saying, and will repeat later, is that we have had Spirit around us our whole lives. Once we become aware of this, we need to remember that fact because I feel we are in danger of getting carried away in some cases, thinking that Spirits have just started being around you, or you have summoned them in some cases. The fact is you are just more aware now, so there is no reason, in my opinion, to change anything drastically. That is unless you are an arsehole, but that would need changing regardless of an awakening, wouldn't it?

I want to demonstrate how dangerous it can be going for readings and hearing information that may not be correct, by using examples of readings I have given that I nearly got wrong or could have easily misinterpreted. However, simply saying what I saw rather than try to interpret anything saved the embarrassment, hurt, or worse. So often I pass things that make no sense at all to me, and all I can do is trust that the client will understand.

The information we are trusted to pass to clients in psychic mediumship readings can, quite literally, be life or death situations. I attended a LOT of readings myself whilst I was going through all of this, and some of the things I was told were dangerous. I ended up so confused about what to believe that I hit an extremely low period in my life and even at one point questioned the whole point of life, something that so many others I know have struggled with during an awakening.

This book of ramblings and gripes won't explain the mysteries of the universe (well, it might, but that's a far stretch even for someone as opinionated as me). What it might do is explain in detail how I navigated this awakening with a view of questioning everything I was told and only trusting what I could demonstrate and confirm for myself.

Again, not much I say here I tell as fact, so I encourage you to listen to the way I see things along with the reasons why I have come to certain conclusions. Just because we are having an awakening, it does not mean we have to remove the need for rational thinking because maybe, just maybe, this unregulated industry could have lots of scammers and bullshiters trying to blend in with the hard-working, talented Spirit workers who, unfortunately, find their work harder as a result. We look everywhere for answers when this all starts happening and, like it or not, there are people who know that, just waiting to rip us off.

Very important to add is that I am not special or doing anything exceptional. These are not superpowers; these are a part of every human body that I believe have started waking up in us more over the last few decades. Whilst remaining very open-minded, it's important I stay grounded and put my sceptical head back on just to make sure I have evidence before I make my mind up about anything. If there is no evidence, I cannot follow blindly, and for that reason, I fear I sometimes come across as ignorant with my views, so please be warned and try not to take offence. It is not anything more than needing things to make perfect sense for the sake of my mental health.

Traditions and teachings we learn throughout life are passed on and passed on again through generations, often without evidence. We have no real way of knowing what fact is, or what may just be rumour or hearsay. Months of searching for answers and making sense of what was going on with me was a challenging time and, although I will try, it will be difficult to put into words fully.

I'm sure if you are reading this and have read other books and articles looking for answers, you will have at times read something that makes perfect sense. You may then have read something else from the same person and thought, *That sounds a bit crazy, what the hell am I thinking? This is all crazy, forget it*. There is a reason for that, and I feel the biggest issue with getting our heads around this whole subject is a lot of the fear, and, to a certain extent, threats, that subconsciously, mankind plants into one another's minds.

Now, I know for an absolute fact that I am certainly not the only person who has wrestled with their sanity over this. I have had many clients so scared to sit with me for a reading because they worry that something they say will sound crazy, with no one around them to talk to about anything they are experiencing for fear of sounding like they are losing the plot.

At the same time, they have tried to talk about this to many people in this world of Spiritualism who have, at times, filled their heads with fear and rubbish.

Very often a client has been fed so much bullshit that they will fear opening up the gates of hell to demons or whatever you want to call it, and it's completely laughable. At the same time, it is so sad that we let this affect us to the point of suicide in some cases. Yes, suicide! This is not being overdramatic; I have had many clients that are suicidal thinking they are losing the plot and it is shocking to hear some of the things they were told. This is why we as Spirit workers, lightworkers, mediums, psychics, or whatever you want to call us need to be so careful that what we are passing is nothing but FACT. Not our facts or beliefs but the smells, images, words, and feelings that are presented and nothing more.

No Spirit worker has the right to tell you something is absolute truth without a relevant explanation or demonstration. Trying to make your mind go along with something that does not make sense will just make you tired and sceptical, and you have every right to be, because you have common sense and a questioning mind so never feel you can't use it! Remove the fear and rather than trust what I am saying, just see if you see any logic in my explanations; then make up your own mind.

Although I consider myself religious in my own way, my stubbornness will not allow me just to believe what is written in a book without having some sort of demonstration, BUT I do believe in a greater good or higher being. As far as I know that greater good and higher being could simply be the good within oneself. I'm a good person anyway as far as I know, so why would I need to follow commandments that I would have thought were just normal human rules?

There is a comedian called Jim Jefferies and although he can be quite offensive, I do find a lot of what he says very funny because I have a dark sense of humour. I was watching a stand-up routine of his one day a few years ago and he started talking about religion. Although this was comedy and meant for a laugh, something he said completely summed up the main message for me when it comes to religion.

Now, again, if you don't like swearing or bad language, this may not be the book for you, but I have to include the following quote, word for word. YOU HAVE BEEN WARNED!

He was talking about the Bible and the fact that it's too wordy and it does not need to be all that detailed to get us to behave in a way that should just come naturally to us.

> **"As humans we should not need instructions on how to behave as good people."**

Good point, but the following words struck a chord with me…

> **"The Bible should be one sheet of paper, and on that sheet of paper, it should say… Try not to be a Cunt… And if you do that every day, you'll be a good person."**

For me, it sums it all up, just this short line out of a comedy segment. I hope that if God does exist, he will understand and accept that he gave me a brain and common sense, so I will use that to make sense of things I am told. Because of that, how can he expect me not to use the brain he gifted me with to question something I have seen no proof of? In fact, the one thing that stands out to me with religion is a lot of war and conflict. Not to mention the church being one of the biggest and richest (combined) corporations in the world, and I am sure that there is something in the Bible about Jesus getting angry about a church being used for business…

I cannot remember now, but who cares? As long as nobody runs out of £20s on a Sunday when the donation basket comes round, why should we question anything! If we query the framework and why the church is such a cash-rich business, possibly taking away from the reason they are there in the first place, then we are just defamatory or slanderous to even mention such a thing. I cannot help but to question the current narrative and wonder if humans have somehow changed it from the original, possibly over hundreds of years.

Surely we are allowed to believe in a greater good while at the same time, question the effect human intervention has had on the details over the years. Let's face it, us humans are good at ruining good things sometimes, just look at the state of the planet!

Keeping in mind that God gave us common sense, why are we killing each other over the subject of religion, and causing more division than most other subjects over the years? He must be looking down at us as a race just thinking,

What on earth are these people doing?

I also see a large amount of hypocrisy surrounding religion for various reasons on a personal level, both in my life and with people I have encountered. There is a song called "Never Went to Church" by The Streets, written about the death of Mike Skinner's (lead) father and how he felt he needed to pray when things were hard after losing his dad. A particular line in that song reminds me of all the times I used to pray to God in my head when I was in trouble.

"Please God, don't let me run out of fuel before the services". But when I was fine, and everything was going my way, I didn't pray at all. What a hypocrite!

The line is this...

> **"I never cared about God when life was sailing on the calm, so I said I'd get my head down and deal with this ache in my heart. And for that, if God exists, I reckon he'd pay me regard."**

I'm sure that if we try to be good people, learn from our mistakes, treat others, this earth, and all its inhabitants with respect, we'll do OK by him.

Not feeling religious in the typical sense does not have to make me ungrateful to Spirit, just curious about what humans may have done with the story through the ages. However, there is one question that I would love to ask God if he does exist. A question that, while it remains unanswered, makes me question the whole point of religion. A question that someone will have a smart-arse answer for no doubt, but I don't think any answer could help me TRULY understand this.

If you were the creator and made all this; if you can save and heal like I was taught, please, please, please explain to me this: Why do so many people, even children, have to go through so much suffering and pain? Why would that pain, at times, be in the name of religion? Why also would you let people go through the torment of losing a loved one, with no idea of what happens after they pass, but only allow your followers to speak to the almighty? In fact, is this hell? Is that the big joke? Have us humans really got the wrong end of the stick?

Yes, I'm sure there is a more detailed explanation for that, but I really do have to ask. Personally, I say thanks to Spirit in my way and will continue to do so until I have it proven to me that I need to be in church every Sunday, saying thank you to a God that as far as I know, might just be someone's messed up story. Not blindly accepting something that doesn't make sense is something I feel that neither I nor anyone else should feel shame over. It's just me making use of the common sense 'God' apparently gifted me.

I had an experience during a reading within the last year that completely stunned me. Something that I was glad received so much validation from the client. I was talking to a lady whose father had passed away and she was very nervous. This was because he was a priest and apparently would have been very much against her seeing a medium, believing the only Spirit we should talk to is the almighty. The worry of what she had been taught all her life made her feel such mixed emotions. These were deep, lifelong fears affecting many areas of the life she should have been happy to live, certainly not anxious or in fear, like this.

At the time I was unaware of the details; I just had a lady sitting there asking me for a reading, so after greeting her and explaining to her how I worked, a gentleman came through. He had a very jolly feeling and was on my right-hand side, so for that reason I knew this was a blood relative. I have two corridors on my right-hand side (I will explain in detail later), but when someone comes through on the first corridor, I have a maternal blood relative. On the second corridor, I have a paternal blood relative. The closeness of the male on the paternal corridor on my right-hand side told me this blood relative was a recent passing and that he was either a father or grandfather.

He was giving me an almost awkward feeling but in a funny way that told me he had a sense of humour, and this joke, he wanted me to know, was on him! I described what he was wearing and, yes, it was clear this male was her father, showing me his "workwear," and then what came next was clear...

"This is awkward!" were the words that came through clearly.

After that, I was shown more evidence, like the pets they had and details of events and timelines (I feel it is so important to give enough evidence to make what I say mean something). I had these words with a big grin come through as clear as anything from her father. All that fear and worry she had because of what she had learned throughout life was unnecessary! Something I think, is a great shame.

Obviously, that wasn't the unlocking of the secrets of the universe, but it sure made that lady lose a huge weight off her shoulders, with enough evidence for her to leave the reading knowing I wasn't throwing vague words and hoping they stuck. She knew I couldn't have known the things I said, and I'm grateful to her dad for that.

I never do well; I just sit and say what I see. Spirit does well using energy and tools to get this to us to pass on, and that man in Spirit gave so much evidence that day, even correcting things while she was talking. Things like, "My dad had four boxes of tools", while talking about him and then him correcting it so I could say, "He said five boxes, there is one in the back of his car too under a green blanket" (she messaged me the next day to confirm this was correct).

The thing about this that stood out for me, is the fact that I had a male come through that had spent his whole life with the belief that we are only supposed to speak to the almighty, and not family in Spirit. Now bearing in mind this was someone that devoted his life to the church; after he passed, the love for his daughter was clear as anything. The lifelong belief was resulting in such fear within his daughter because she was apparently not following the rules he thought were so important! What a shame it is to spend your life in fear, just because of something you were told, but saw no proof of!

If something does not come through detailed, I will try not to pass on the vague. Someone coming to hear from a lost relative and me just saying they are there, and they love and support you, as far as I'm concerned, leaves more doubt than anything and if that's all I can say with no evidence, I refund, simple as that.

Someone coming for a reading to hear from a lost relative, getting told detailed information like what car they had, how many children, current events they have seen since passing, even something as silly as them saying that the person I'm reading for has just ordered a pizza can be what makes this so valuable for the client. That pizza thing really happened during a Zoom reading, but I said, "You have a pizza in your oven." I mean it was close, but the client corrected me to say she had just ordered one. It was still a validation but with a slight mistake.

Her pizza was in the oven, no doubt, but not in her house—another lesson for me, reminding me to say only what I saw! I was shown a pizza being put into an oven and PRESUMED it was her oven. It wasn't. A very small detail in this circumstance, but it could be a very big detail in certain circumstances, and a reminder for me to only ever SAY WHAT I SEE, with no presumptions.

It took me a long time, coming from an engineering background, where everything is methodical and easy to follow, to accept I was having a "Spiritual Awakening" and going through what, let's be honest, can be a right pain in the arse. One where on occasion I just felt I wanted to be ignorant again, not having to deal with so many conflicting words of advice.

But was I ever ignorant? Was this why I felt so out of place in life, always trying to fit a mould? Why is everything so fear-based? What is really going on with all this? Is it something to do with my past?

Well, I could look to my past, I suppose...

2.

MY 'NORMAL' LIFE

My best childhood memories before high school all revolve around being in the back of Mum's car during the night on the way to Cornwall to see my nan and gramps. They ran a pizza parlour in Carbis Bay and even though it was an eight-hour drive because the roads were not as good as they are now, I loved it. I loved going there in the holidays and even thinking back on it makes me emotional. All of it was great, but two things stand out for me massively now. Two places in Cornwall used to make me feel very strange as a young boy for reasons I do not know, almost a rush of emotion type feeling.

One of these places was Land's End, with the visitors' centre and the cliffs with crosses marking lives that had been lost to the sea. I was quite young but can remember the strange feeling as I walked around the centre, listening to stories of the sea and how no man can tame her, even though so many lives have been lost trying.

Come to think of it, when getting to Cornwall, nearly at Nan's, we used to see who could see the sea first. Even seeing the sea used to give me that strange feeling that I can't explain.

The other place was Lizard Point—cliffs, dangerous tides, and a stony bit of a beach that is more of a dog-walking spot than a tourist beach. The stories of lost lives on information boards and warnings about how rough the sea can be were something I couldn't get enough of. It amazed me that the sea has such power. I could stare at it for ages and get lost thinking about all the events that have taken place at that spot that I was unaware of and the stories that the land could tell. My whole life I have wanted to live near the sea and hopefully one day that will happen, but for now, like my whole life, I am very much inland.

The other thing I think of when I look back now as a five-year-old is all the gift shops; I was absolutely fascinated with amethyst. I remember always asking for some, and I'm sure Mum just thought I'd end up losing something that, for a bit of rock, is very expensive, especially in a gift shop in a tourist spot. It's not the sort of thing you see in the supermarket, or the Arndale Centre in Luton, and it wasn't like I could jump on eBay or Etsy in the late eighties and early nineties!

I have no idea why and could never remember the other stones on display, I just wanted amethyst. I want it and I'm five years old, so I will keep asking, ruin your day, and maybe tomorrow, when I start asking again, you will cave. I do remember coming home with a lump of rough-cut amethyst one day though, in a little plastic box, so apparently, she did cave. But she was right too; I did lose it!

These memories had no significance until later in life when my awakening began. It's clearer now, the emotions near the sea and the reminders of lives lost to it, the need to have amethyst, ignoring the hundreds of other stones in the shops, it all had meaning. As I will explain later, during an awakening I feel it's important to look back at things that you didn't really think about to see if they become relevant.

I grew up in a town called Luton, around 30 minutes north of London. Life was straightforward (ish), although I spent a lot of it miserable for various reasons. I put that down to the fact that I was "oversensitive", an "overthinker" or took things "too seriously" (ish) because that's what I was always told at school or by people around me. I still hear it even to this day, but this is not the fault of anyone at all. I do overthink; I am extremely sensitive; I am too serious or, in contrast, a complete clown if the pendulum swings.

Naturally evolving to avoid the bullying, I learned the way of getting through life was to be that clown, a complete clown, and care about nothing at all. Or at least pretend to, and this worked well. I seemed to get bullied less so I went with it. What made that way of living easier was the fact that I could not get my head around having to sit in a school and do what someone else told me was essential to my future, so I had plenty of chances to play the clown. I can't describe the feeling of anxiety, being that age, feeling like I was wasting time sitting there watching life pass by when there was so much I wanted to do, and it wasn't that! I did have a love for two subjects though...

Maths, because you can't argue with maths. Even I can't question it, and you know exactly where you stand with the teacher because there is no room for anything to be lost in translation or for anyone's theory to get in the way of fact. (Unless you are my daughter and want to start splitting hairs! She must take after me.)

Science by default is not always "exact science" and is all about questioning and proving old science wrong, so I loved that too! I'm sure I could have done well in my exams had I stayed at school, but in my head, it was the principle of it. I have no idea why I had this problem with being told what to do as a young kid, but I was independent, or at least as independent as a kid my age could be.

I really was annoyed about it at the time… How dare they tell me what would shape my future when I had, during my high school years, been working three paper rounds, working night shifts as a controller in a taxi rank (minicab office), and dragging an old baby changing unit (it was sort of like a table when it folded out) to the local car boot sale every Sunday. I was there at the crack of dawn to sell whatever I could find going cheap after I had a walk round while other sellers were setting up. I would grab the early bargains and mark the price up a bit before placing them for sale on my stall.

I shape my future and I want to work hard. I love learning and researching, but only when I choose to and in subjects I'm interested in at the time. That isn't stubbornness or being defiant; that's just my brain shutting off if something doesn't feel necessary or interesting to me. To be clear, these were my thoughts at the time, and, looking back, I wish I had finished school and not been such a strong-willed kid.

This was at the age of around 13 years old and in my head, I could be out delivering flyers or selling something, but these bastards had me sitting there in an RE or history lesson. So I bunked off, and if I wasn't bunking, I was disruptive, or daydreaming, or looking at girls (and getting told to grow up a lot by girls) or talking about anything apart from what I was supposed to be, or maybe planning what I would do after school to make money and prove these arseholes wrong.

During some of the boring lessons, I just left the room after registration and joined a more interesting class where I could find someone as disruptive as me to have a giggle with, like Graham and Neil, because they were always game for having a laugh and messing around. When that got boring, I would just turn up for register then walk straight back out again, thinking I was the next Richard Branson, heading back to my house to plan my empire because Mum trusted me with my own key and she was at work until the end of the school day working her arse off to build some security for her family after the divorce.

My dad had been made bankrupt for various reasons and was taken to court for £2 million so the house my mum and dad built had to be sold. Dad was back at his childhood home with his father. Mum, my sister, and me were thrown into emergency accommodation but Mum worked hard and got a deposit together to buy her house in Cannon Lane.

As I was saying…

One day, while I was in school, I was dragged out of class for messing around, nothing too bad, just talking or not concentrating, something like that. The teacher who dragged me outside said the following:

> **"You will be on benefits for the rest of your life anyway so you don't need to worry about any of this; you can sit out here while everyone else learns."**

That was that! These are some of the most memorable words said to me in my entire life. Right or wrong, my thought at the time, was this...

> **"Fuck you and this entire system! Who the hell has the right to tell me what my future holds?"**

What I was oblivious to was the fact that being a complete clown was a mask for a shit ton of emotional crap that was really messing me up and nothing to do with me being independent. I couldn't have been further from independent. I have always been more practical than academic, taking things to bits, fixing things, and that is why being an electro-mechanical engineer suits me. But that's not the reason I was so depressed, surely? Mum and Dad were divorced, but that wasn't the reason either; half the school's parents were divorced, and they were fine, so that wasn't a reason to be feeling the way I did.

So why was I in such a state when I was on my own, worrying about anything and everything that could go wrong with everything? I hated the thought of sleep and the thought of waking up in the morning having to deal with people, leaving the safety of my room where I was just me without pressure to fit into a life that I had no control over and was frightened of. No one knew I was so scared of life and leaving the house because while trying to convince the world you are happy, you can become a brilliant actor.

This all becomes relevant later in this book so stick with it.

My dad lived about an hour away then. He'd taken on a lease for a pub with a lady he was seeing called Carol. Carol was just a scary lady to me at that time who ran the Parrot public house in Farley Hill, Luton when they first met each other. That place was rough, and you had to be scary to run it. She ended up leaving there, to start a life with my dad, in Shepshed, Leicestershire.

I saw Dad during the school holidays and loved getting a few days with him every now and again, a bonus too that he ran a pub, it was great!

I loved listening to the jukebox downstairs while I was upstairs getting ready to go to bed. Hearing muffled ballads playing with the whole pub singing along was a good feeling. That drunken sing-along at the end of the night at closing time gave me that strange feeling like I used to get in Cornwall looking at the sea.

Carol and my dad spent most nights splitting up fights and trying to stop windows or chairs from getting broken, but there was a period of time before that, somewhere between "a few beers after a long day" and "one too many beers, leading to local rivalries erupting," when everyone was enjoying themselves that just felt good. I lay upstairs in bed listening to muffled ballads, tearing up for no reason at all and feeling waves of emotion that I was really confused about. I just didn't know why!

I remember one night, a song called "Nightswimming" by R.E.M. came on the jukebox. That string intro then most of the pub singing along while someone on the other side of the pub was having a punch-up (I heard another window getting smashed. It even got to the stage that the windows by the pool table were bricked up to save the hassle of replacing them all the time.)

I got so emotional for some reason; that song, all that happiness, and my dad that to be fair, hadn't seen us as much as he could have after the divorce, so I'd missed him. The punch-up was irrelevant, it didn't matter those two drunken idiots were fighting; that's just what happened in that pub. I had no idea why I was so emotional though, and it was something I spent a lot of time thinking about. I don't think I felt sad, I don't know what I was feeling at all. But I know I'm oversensitive; that's just me.

(The pub at the time was the Red Lion, in a small town called Shepshed, Leicestershire.)

A year or two later, in 1999, at around the age of 15, while I was busy avoiding school, looking for ways to make money and build my future empire, I got into trouble doing something I shouldn't have been doing with mobile phones. It involved taking them apart and soldering a chip into them to make the available balance infinite and, needless to say, they were selling like hotcakes. I sold a lot of these to a lot of dodgy characters, and I was RAKING it in! That's until BT Cellnet (as it was called at the time) decided to turn all my dodgy phones off at once.

For legal reasons, this part of the book is fiction! This never happened, officer.

At that point, I had a lot of people wanting refunds and a LOT of threats! I had to get out of Luton fast. I had always been a bit of an arse, but the sort of trouble I got into was the sort of trouble that any teacher telling me off would really have to try not to laugh while doing so. I was a clown but a harmless clown, not nasty (I hope!). One example…

One day, my science teacher, Dr Noakes, was giving a talk and had our class of around 30 children bring our chairs and sit around his desk so we could see the board behind him as there was a lot of small writing and it was a dusty blackboard because we were in the old part of the school still. A friend (Graham) and I played a game that involved a task every time Dr Noakes turned his back to write on the board. We'd take it in turns to get up quickly and move his pot plant from the back of his desk about one inch at a time towards the front and sit down again before he turned back round to face us, explaining what he had been writing meant. Over that half hour, we slowly edged the plant forward without getting caught until it was right at the front edge of his desk. It was a massive plant too, so I don't know how he didn't notice. It was now my turn again, and he turned his back once again to write something else on the board.

I jumped up and pushed the plant… No desk left, so the plant crashed onto the floor. He spun around to see his lovely plant on the floor and soil everywhere with me leaning over his desk like a rabbit caught in headlights and the whole class laughing at the fact that I was caught red-handed.

He dragged me out of class and as I was explaining what the game was, I could see him doing everything he could not to laugh so he could give me the telling off I needed. Very childish but certainly not nasty and, just so you know, the plant was fine after it was put back in the pot.

Back to the trouble with the phones…

This was all too much now; I was in trouble and needed to get away from Luton. I did not need a psychic to tell me that I had to leave, FAST! Meanwhile, my dad had since left the pub he was in to move down to Harefield in Greater London. This was to take on a new, larger pub that Carol and he really liked. It was a bit smarter, and as they were looking to quieten down a bit, it suited them that they were taking on a food pub that was **likely** to involve less bar fights than the boozer they had just left, but it certainly had its moments when the fair came to town.

Feeling the danger I would be in if I stayed in Luton, and equally fed up with school, I left before any exams took place and went to live with Dad at the new pub. Lesson learned and time to grow up, I had a lot to prove now! I was later told that someone in Luton was paid £500 to stab me over the phone thing. Although it was quite serious, I had to laugh at the low price. I do know now that the person I was told had been paid the £500 was more than capable. In fact, 22 years later, looking back, it was probably the best move I could have made at the time.

Life at the pub was so different; I was new there. I wasn't Sean, the geek that got bullied and was naughty. I was the boss' son in Dad's pub. We agreed to say that I was 18 to everyone so that I could get away with working behind the bar. I think because Carol and Dad were worried that I would be a dosser (lazy scrounger), they were trying to get me working where they could keep an eye on me, but I loved it. I've only learned to sit still at weekends during the last six years, so dosser was very unlikely, but I was more than happy to suddenly be three years older and working behind the bar.

Carol's nephew Clive (my step-cousin) also lived at the pub. He was a bit of a handful and spent a lot of his time fighting during his younger days. After getting out of prison with nowhere to go, Carol and my dad said he could stay with us for a couple of weeks. He was still there two years later and ended up being more of a surrogate older brother to me before being sent back to jail over yet another fight in a pub one night. I owe him a lot because, along with my dad, he massively helped with increasing my confidence and I certainly did not have that "scared little boy" feeling that I had through childhood. Clive went back to Luton in the end and started a family, living a much calmer life, certainly a different person compared to the handful he was 22 years ago!

During my time working at the pub, I learned how to deal with people, talk to people from different walks of life, and become an artist! I treated bar work as a performance (the confidence certainly sorted itself out!); pouring five drinks simultaneously became an art of which I was proud. I loved it that customers would want to be served by me because I treated it as an art, making that boring process interesting for them.

My new confidence and social skills felt so natural, like I was free from the school system and now part of an environment that I fit into. I felt comfortable and relaxed, knowing I was earning a wage whilst learning about life. This was in my blood. I could get to know so many people, learn about how different people get through life, and see how people from different classes interact.

Looking back now, I went from the person who hated leaving my bedroom for fear of being bullied and getting told I was a failure to then come into this new life and fitting in like it was the most natural thing for me. It was all because my mind just hated the thought of being told how to behave in a system that made no sense to me, like my time was being wasted and even at that young age, the thought of time passing by and being wasted, filled me with such anxiety. It makes me so sad for the so-called "naughty kids" or "misfits" that are stuck in a system their brains simply cannot gel with.

For me, the real learning never stops; the learning about life and how to live it; the learning about how to adapt and behave in certain situations; the learning about morals and why we CHOOSE to be good people. If you don't choose to be a good person and just do it because you are told to or think you should, I feel you become fake and confused, lost in a way. Learning why we need to be good people is what makes our souls evolve.

I am sure I'm supposed to say that everyone needs education, and everyone must flow through the system to ensure a good future, but I can't. Instead, I will be honest and stand by what I truly feel, and it is as simple as this:

Most kids will do fine at school and, yes, we need to be educated to have the best possible chance of achieving all we can in life. BUT when you get a kid who has a brain that cannot compute things the way they are told it should and he starts acting out, looks like he is just being a pain in the arse, do not presume he is just a waste of space. That kid's mind may well be running all over the place with world-changing ideas and solutions and at the same time thinking they are failing at everything, sinking lower than most people could imagine.

I was lucky to have somewhere to go and this clean start, but I have absolutely no doubt whatsoever that had I stayed in the system that convinced me I was a failure before I had even started because I didn't fit that mould, I would be in prison or possibly dead by now. Suicide, crime, or Mr Hitman would have got me I suppose, and all three of those scenarios would have been a result of the fact that I was not coping in that system. In turn that led me to do other things without direction or support from a system that has no alternative route for kids who think differently. I was not a bad kid at all, my mum had taught me morals as well as how to be respectful, and had I been more open with her about my feelings, maybe it would have been different.

I was just thinking in a different way and felt trapped in a system that was wasting my time. Let's be honest; nowadays, I would be told I had a condition or something and given drugs to cure my 'illness' so I would just conform to that system. This thought becomes ironic later in the book!

All of this, why? Because a single system cannot work for everyone. All we do is convince a shit load of mostly bright kids who just think a bit differently that they are complete failures and have no hope. What happens next? Drink? Drugs? Suicide? Unfortunately, we become what we are taught we are unless we have a stroke of luck. It's a shame to think about what could have been, for so many, if there was a system in place to take the kids who don't fit one particular system and nurture what works for them instead of installing a will to fail in their heads; unintentionally most of the time, of course, but still damaging.

My mum unfortunately had no idea I was this bad. I had become an expert actor and had everyone convinced I was just a typical naughty teen. I know this is a book about awakenings and mental health, but all this is needed and will fall into place later, I promise! I find myself apologising a lot still and explaining myself. I will explain this fear of being judged in more detail, but for now I will try to sum up the years between then and my awakening so I can get on with this.

While living at the pub, I ended up getting a job as a trainee engineer for a company that was run by one of our regulars. The work was good for me because I was driving to different sites and fixing things. Between that and one other company that was the same job, I spent four years learning, before starting my own company in 2007. At around the same time, in 2007, I met my soon-to-be-wife, Victoria, and soon after, came our two children. Carol sadly lost her battle with cancer in January of 2012, and my dad, five years later in April of 2017, lost his fight with leukaemia. Clive and I sat with Dad on his last night and we both agreed it just felt like he wanted to be with Carol now because he had waited long enough. In a way, I feel like my dad gave up on life the day Carol died, but he was a good actor, like me.

Due to the events in that period of time, and although I was unaware of it, I think 2017 was the start of my awakening; the time that the Spirit around me felt like they needed to step things up and try to get my attention.

It took a lot longer than that before I realised how differently I was behaving though; I didn't realise I was such a grumpy arsehole...

EDIT: On the evening of March 7th, 2022, during the final the final stages of checking and preparing this book for release, I was sitting at my desk and received a call to be told that Clive's life had been suddenly cut short earlier that day. He was one of the toughest men I have ever known, and although he had his troubles in his younger years, he always had family at his core and was the first to make sure everyone around him was safe and confident in life. Along with my dad, he taught me to keep my head up no matter what I was facing and gave me the mindset to never again be a 'victim'. I just wish one of us had picked up the phone.

Hopefully hear from you soon, mate.

Clive Brown 1967 – 2022

3.

A MISERABLE AWAKENING

Just at the start of my awakening, I had apparently turned into a grumpy, negative, suspicious, and basically horrible person to be around. That and the fact that I was now on the wrong side of 35 certainly didn't help.

I stopped finding things in life satisfying and nothing made me happy. Some people I had known for years suddenly appeared to me as complete strangers. I'm a people pleaser, some would say to keep myself busy helping everyone else to save me from dealing with my own crap or just from an inbuilt need to be wanted and appreciated. I don't know how exactly, but people around me were changing. People I had known for so long were making me feel tired and I was getting angrier and angrier with the way people acted. With that, I was seeing words come out of some people's mouths and they were empty; I could see fake sincerity. It was like the mask was slipping down and that fake nice, warm personality was just a robot with no depth. How were people suddenly feeling empty to me? Not everyone of course, just some of them.

At the same time, I started feeling like I had "something" around me. A feeling I could not explain at the time, but it was like my thoughts were louder, pointing things out that I hadn't noticed, then when I checked, my thoughts were correct. I was genuinely worried about my mental state, and it got worse by the day.

I went from wanting so many people around, bending over backwards to help anyone at all, to suddenly wanting to cut people out of my life because I thought they were sucking away my energy. I became bitter and angry, feeling like so many people around me had used me for everything they needed, and when it came to me needing help, I had nowhere near as many friends. The thing is I did not really ask for help, I was just hoping I wouldn't need to because I was being so stubborn. Who would understand what

I was talking about? And would they just tell me I was losing the plot?

Eventually I realised that it was me changing, not the world around me, and yes, these people did care, but my consciousness train just pulled away, and I had to hold the brakes on so hard to slow myself down to my old pace that it became more exhausting by the day. I just wanted to be alone and have time with myself to work out if I was having a midlife crisis or a breakdown or whatever the hell was going on with me. I think 'Empty' would be a good description.

Suddenly, things I was previously happy to do, I developed a hate for. I could not sit in front of the TV without getting huge waves of anxiety (I still get that now). "How can I sit here when while my life drains away with every tick I hear on that wall clock?" I could be reading, learning things, doing something. I felt like I was wasting every second of my life and blaming everyone around me for not filling this big void I now had.

The next day could be the opposite, loving everyone around me, convinced I'd had a crazy day yesterday and "What comes over me when I start thinking we have Spirit around us anyway? Am I losing the plot? Do I need a holiday? What is going on with me? I'm sorry, that won't happen again. Of course I'm happy... What's on TV?"

But it did happen again. And again. I was like Jeckel and Hyde, two different people from one day to the next, wrestling with what the world said was crazy and what I felt strongly was not so crazy.

It wasn't long before I ended up living in a house on my own. For the first time in my whole life, I was alone; alone in a strange house with my own head for company and it was the first time in my life that I knew what silence really was. Instantly, from the first night I spent in that house, I knew I was not alone. My fridge freezer has a big clunky switch at the top of it that says, "Super Freeze" on it, something I noticed but had no need ever to switch on. The decoration was old and dated but the feeling I got when I sat there at night on my own was very strange, like I was OK being on my own. I didn't feel lonely; I didn't feel scared; I didn't feel much other than hairs sporadically standing up all over my body for no reason at all.

Every morning, when I came downstairs for the first four to six months, I was greeted with the downstairs toilet door open and my fridge switched to super freeze. So many pictures on my phone were of that super freeze switch at bedtime and videos of me closing that door and rattling it to be sure it was closed. The biggest shock to me was the fact that I felt no fear whatsoever with that going on. Even now I can remember before it stopped happening, walking down the stairs, familiar with it and wondering if it was going to have happened again.

It is funny looking back now because I really missed the switch thing on the fridge when it stopped happening. It was like whoever it was did not want to play anymore and got bored. I realise now that it stopped as soon as I started paying attention, so why would Spirit need to put that much energy into getting my attention now that I could tune in?

While all this was going on back then I started scrying, trying Spirit boxes, dowsing rods and anything else I could think of to see what the Spirits in this house were trying to tell me. Was there something urgent I needed to know? A warning about someone around me? Why else would they be trying to get my attention if it wasn't a warning?

One night, I remember letting my dog out the back to do his dog business; it was dark but I knew the back gate was always shut so just opened the door and let him out without looking, while I went back into the kitchen to finish making my dinner. A few seconds after letting him out, as I got to the kitchen door, I heard the words, "WHY IS THE BACK GATE OPEN?" as clear as anything in my right ear, like someone had said the words right next to my face. I went back to check in the garden and the back gate was open, with the dog now gone.

It was pitch black out, but I somehow knew what direction to go and walked straight into someone's front garden down the road to find him there. A Spirit helped me out, and I know that because the gate was never left open. I had no idea why it was that day, but I'm guessing there'd been someone snooping around or a delivery driver looking for another house. Also, there is no way I would have known what garden he was in, out of all the other gardens around this house, yet I walked straight to the one he was in, passing 10–15 other houses on the way. Whoever was giving me this warning, just helped me with a day-to-day task that could have turned into a nightmare for me and the dog that night.

It is crazy looking back now over my life at how many times I have been helped out but just had no idea. This time, though, Spirit made sure that voice would be heard loud and clear, so as not to be confused with me just talking to myself. Angel work, demonstrated perfectly in day-to-day life. There was still doubt though, I could have just been losing my mind for all I knew, I needed more!

I started going online to forums, psychic mediums, and anyone at all who could answer my question. "Who is here around me and what is the warning?" I got far too hung up on it being some kind of warning for me. A few, but not many, brought through a few family members and that was lovely. Some tried to arrange meeting me for sex, and, although flattering, that was not overly helpful. Some told me I needed to sage my house because the Spirits there were evil and the house needed cleansing. But I felt relaxed and didn't feel in danger in the slightest so automatically took that as bullshit.

Has anyone got "Killed by a ghost" on their death certificate? Just one is all I need to prove me wrong, "Killed by a Spirit," anyone?

And back up a minute… "Did you say sage? Sage the herb? Sage that grows in the garden, used in cooking? WHAT THE FUCK IS THAT GOING TO DO?"

"So SAGE is going to save me from the devil? I thought evil Spirits were supposed to be dangerous? With the devil or demons or whatever that rubbish is that you are spouting, the key to my safety is SAGE?" I can't even get my head around it just for negative human energy either because the smell of burnt sage certainly isn't my first choice of aromatherapy and is more likely to just piss me off as much as the suggestion of it did.

Call me a sceptic or naïve, but I have never heard anything so ridiculous in my life as burning sage to rid a house of evil. And this is coming from someone who keeps lemons around the house to absorb negative human energy. Lemons rot in angry rooms; they dry and go hard in happy rooms. Try it for yourself!

Anyway, this fear we have thrown at us, about how to be careful and how dangerous an evil Spirit is, just does not add up for me. I'm sure me saying that will result in someone trying to educate me on the history of why we use sage, and it will be very well explained, I'm sure. Unfortunately, that would be entertaining even the thought of an evil or negative Spirit and it's something I just don't accept. It would just be one human passing fear to another human like we have done for centuries, and, frankly, my opinion is that it's complete bollocks!

Let's think logically about this...

If a negative Spirit can be warded off by a protection prayer or a herb out of the garden, how dangerous do you really think that negative Spirit is? Do you honestly think it sounds plausible that something that is apparently so dangerous and needs so much protection against can be tamed with these silly practices? It kind of makes a mockery of the words "evil" and "dangerous", don't you think?

It is almost just like a symbolic suggestion, or 'signal' if anything, like a way to tell Spirit to "Fuck off." If that is the case, I'll just say that instead if required and save my money.

What is it with us humans and the need to instil fear? Always a threat of danger from something that has not been proven to us. In fact, the more I hear things like this the more it is clear that as a race, we are fantastic at spreading fear. Most of the situations we are fearful of have not even been proven, let alone ever happened! So often we are told that 'physical' things are just here on Earth and that we're just light when we die. So how can we take something earthly and physical like fire and make hell for people that worship the wrong god, or misbehave?

Could it be possible that any fear we hold is nothing more than a result of humans telling stories to keep control of other humans? Could there actually be a chance that wrongdoings and earthly stuff just stays here, giving us something we must deal with in our souls when we no longer have the physical stuff to keep us busy? Could all the horror films, stories in books, and fear of having to rid ourselves of evil Spirits just be in our heads? Could they be fabricated tales to keep people controlled for hundreds of years, generations of deep brainwashing?

"Behave or Santa won't come."

Has anyone got an experience of messing up as a child and Santa not coming, when any other year he did? I'm sure there are exceptions, but again, I think it's fair to be aware that these fears may just be an earthly thing that is used to keep control.

I will repeat this feeling towards the idea of negative Spirit as much as I can because it's something that does us no good whatsoever. In fact, I have seen this fear destroy people. The reason I feel so strongly about it is that during my work as a medium, I have not experienced negative Spirits at all. I have experienced very scary events, but all through fear of us here, not through evil. I have also experienced clients in complete meltdown through a fear of something that they have seen no proof of. Even if evil Spirit does exist, it's the FEAR that does so much more damage!

There have been so many times when a client has asked me why they are being bothered by an evil Spirit and when I look at it deeper, it really isn't the case at all, but any Spirit contact is scary for someone with a life of conditioning to believe in evil. If the Spirit of Mother Teresa woke you up in the middle of the night to give you a hug, with that pre-conditioning, you would probably still panic!

I will ask you to put yourself, for one moment, in the shoes of a Spirit...

You are watching over the person you love, seeing how well things are going. They then hit a point in their life where they feel so low and alone that they are close to the edge. What do you do? Do you try everything to get their attention when they are alone? Do you use every bit of energy you can bring forward to switch the fridge to super freeze? Do you stay with them in the night to try to reassure them they are not as alone as they think? Do you get so desperate because they are on the edge that you start knocking things off worktops just to get them to pay attention to the fact that they are not alone? Everything that could be done would be done to get that person's attention. *That person I love and can't hold because I'm in Spirit, but I'm here, and I'm so desperate for them to know that.* The problem is we have a bottle of Coke fall off the counter and we automatically think the gates of hell have opened and whatever comes out has nothing better to do than play "silly buggers" in our house. I don't see Spirit as anything more than someone who cares about getting your attention when you need someone there or some support. Of course, sometimes some mischief from a Spirit that just has a story to tell because the "light is on". I like to picture any Spirit as an excited puppy; so happy to see you that, yes, they can knock things over and be a bit noisy, but it's only to get your attention, out of love.

"But what about haunted houses?" I have a very detailed view of this type of phenomenon. Actually, I have several views for several scenarios, so I will go into that in far more detail later in the book if I can be bothered to entertain it, but for now, let's say this…

As far as I am concerned, I'm a decent, loving person. I am polite, welcoming, and friendly. If you came to my home, I would welcome you and treat you well. I would talk to you, keep you fed and watered, and generally be a good host. That is unless you came here to get a reaction by provoking me, taunting me, baiting me, and just making yourself a complete pain in the arse. I would certainly ask you to leave, but that may just encourage you to get more of a reaction and you more than likely wouldn't leave because you would be getting a rise out of me or simply couldn't hear me. In that case, I would punch you right in your annoying face! That would not make me evil, would it?

Incidentally, I've watched two separate investigations by two different teams on separate occasions but in the same 'haunted' house. Two completely different perspectives but both with Spirit contact and the difference between the two was simple: Respect and decency. One team went telling Spirit to "Do your worst." Yes, there were some things that got thrown apparently by Spirit, but no one was seriously hurt. The other team went in, sat and asked nicely, respected Spirit and got some of the best physical Spirit interaction I have ever seen. Grumpy Spirit, yes, evil, no!

Back to the story...

I was told to say a protection prayer a lot, and I think this too is a very important subject to talk about. Again, like anything in life, you go for answers but before you get them, you receive a warning and some fear to dwell on. As if an awakening wasn't enough of a confusing time! To be told so often that this protection prayer was so important made no sense to me at all. My kids love it in this house because they feel

Spirit. Although they have never said a protection prayer, they are still alive and have none of the fear that would be needed to be saying a protection prayer in the first place. In fact, I watched my daughter stand in the kitchen one evening and ask Spirit to turn a light off, then back on again. She then walked into the front room after telling me that was "pretty cool" and "nice of them to do that", while asking for some Ben and Jerrys. I stood there gobsmacked but the child that has no influence from fear mongers yet, treated it like the most perfectly normal thing in the world!

I've tried many times since, to get that to happen, but it seems Spirit are happier to entertain children with things like that than they are grown arse men that happen to be mediums!

I was also told that I had guides, angels, and family in Spirit, and that they have protected me from birth. So if the Spirits around me have been protecting me from birth, why now that I have spoken to you, would they not still protect me if I forget to say this silly prayer?

With all that in mind and after all the effort taken by Spirit to get my attention, how dare you suggest the Spirit that is there for ME will disappear if I don't say YOUR prayer! The Spirit around me knows I am a tit, and they are still here, so I will say thank you in my way and not accept someone else putting yet another barrier of fear in front of me in this life; thank you very much!

And we wonder why this world has problems with mental health? With everything we have in life to be worried about, we then get this shit thrown at us too! I have to say here, I realise I probably sound like an arse, but this is honestly what went through my head when I was told these things.

My two kids were here at Halloween because they love the quiet and how they can tune in or use divination or ask Spirit for taps and get two knocks for yes or one for no. (Spirit really do seem to entertain children more than they would for adults!)

One weekend, my son and daughter sat in the lounge while I was busy tidying something up in the kitchen. I walked back into the room to find them both sitting with a candle that was earlier above the fireplace, and a sheet of paper with A–Z on it. Underneath that was a sheet of paper with the words "Flight," "Japan," and "Donald Edwin."

My daughter Eryn was moving the back of the pen across each letter really slowly, and this time, the candle started flickering like crazy at B.

She carried on… "L" "O" "W"—blow.

Why blow? What, blow the candle out?

I did what anyone would do; I sat at my computer and searched the "keywords" that the Spirit had kindly given them. After a while, I came across a website dedicated to servicemen from this area and, after reading through, couldn't believe my eyes! It was one of those points where I just knew there was so much I was yet to learn about all of this.

Donald Edwin Blow was an RAF serviceman, sadly reported missing in Japan in 1942.

He lived down the road from this house and there is absolutely no way on this earth that my children would have known that. The smiles on their faces and the way they said, "Thank you for coming to say hello," were probably the craziest things I have encountered since all this started (well, on par with my daughter telling a light to turn off then back on!). Seeing their natural connection and lack of fear made me extremely proud of them, but still gobsmacked!

Here on Earth, we should focus our fear, not on Spirit but on us. Where there is unhealthy Ego, there is evil. And I certainly haven't witnessed any Ego in Spirit. As explained in the first chapter, I was called an irresponsible father by another light worker for allowing that to happen and not ensuring a circle of protection was in place beforehand. A fucking silly protection circle! I was livid and couldn't let it go...

I asked her if she had kids, and she replied, "Yes." I then asked if her kids had to ask her for protection.

Obviously, she replied, "No." The protection is there out of love, in my opinion. Love is unconditional, making having to ask for protection obsolete, making love unconditional protection by default. Now, I can at least presume there is love here for Spirit to be around and put up with my shit over my whole life, and for that I'm very grateful. It would take an unconditional love to still be here, and I really can't see Spirit not protecting me should I fail to say a silly prayer that feels like someone else's request, not mine.

Again, these are just my views, but my kids certainly have no issues with mental stability and certainly not as much as they would have if I filled their heads with the fear of demons or whatever we need protection from in Spirit. All I have experienced is love, humour, regret, and fear for us here, where all the actual evil and negativity is.

I make no apologies for having no fear of something I cannot see or have seen no proof of. We have enough to fear in day-to-day life, so why would I waste time fearing something I can't compute? All that anxiety for something that makes no sense to me seems completely ridiculous; in fact, stress and anxiety, caused by fear and worry, are huge causes of inflammation or inflammatory cytokines. Inflammation, in one way or another, is the cause of pretty much all diseases, so please tell me, who is the irresponsible one? I stress, just my view; but don't we already have enough to be worried about without worrying about something that has never actually taken up any space on a death certificate?

Back to what I was saying...

As time went on, I was more convinced I was not crazy. But to make sure, I paid a psychiatrist to evaluate me, just in case. Thankfully, though, I was told I was mentally sound. So now I knew I was aware of Spirit, I had to find out more. I wanted to contact Spirit; it was something I became obsessed with. I could feel my hairs standing up and the energy around me change; I was sure I was so close, but I needed to improve on this somehow!

The problem I had was when I watched mediums on TV, I always thought they had a ghost that only they could see standing there having a good old chat. I don't get that so I can't be a medium as I can only feel and I can't see anything, only what I imagine, but that's just my imagination, so I'll ignore that totally because that's silly...

Isn't it?

I'll just carry on writing down what's in my dreams for now because that's what everyone says to do. Although, as with a lot of this, I just have one concern with that. (You can imagine how hard it is to live with me, I watched far too much *Columbo* as a kid!)

So, if I am asleep, and Spirit knows that's the best time to contact me, am I not asleep? And while I'm asleep, if a message does come through, because I have a life of fear in my head and have watched some really good horror films, will my imagination play with that message at all and obscure it somehow? Could that be possible?

I only ask because my dreams start nicely but by the end, I'm in a graveyard running from a clown that's trying to kill me or something like that and is that what Spirit is trying to pass? What does that mean? Could my imagination be jumping in and messing with the original message? Because if that is in any way possible, is it not dangerous, NOT to mention that if we are asking people to journal their dreams? You know, just so they can make their own minds up and not have any unnecessary anxiety?

I'm sure I will get slated for a lot of what I have said here. "Who does he think he is saying this about Spirit workers and the whole basis of my beliefs?"

Like it or not, there is a widely ignored problem with mental health and awakenings, and there are a lot of gaps to fill where things don't make sense. The crap I heard was so damaging to me that if it wasn't for the sake of a few brilliant mediums that I was lucky enough to encounter, I would have walked away from it all convinced that I needed to have a word with myself.

The scariest thing I encountered with some people was the "matter of fact" way I was told a lot of what I now consider to be complete bollocks. The sort of things that if taken seriously enough, could really mess someone's head up. I could have bought all the evil stuff, got scared, warned my kids about the danger of evil Spirit, and given them the same complex around the subject, leaving them to carry on this bullshit way of thinking, that would suggest we should go and see a professional if we want to contact Spirit because it is so dangerous, obviously!

It certainly is a lucky thing for Psychics throughout history, for this narrative of evil to be swallowed up enough to make people think they have to go to a pro, because the dangers they face, should they try to do anything like that themselves, are just not worth the risk. Thankfully though, it is better today than it was in the past.

Please let me make this very clear...

A huge number of Spirit workers have helped me more than I could imagine, and I am so grateful to have met them. So many workers do this with the best intentions, me included. All I am saying is that we need to be careful not to drown in information blindly without making sense of things or it simply won't work out for us over-thinkers.

I do not currently read tarot cards for clients, and I admire anyone who can take all that information and work with it in a talented way. It fascinates me and I do pull the odd card for myself. Sometimes, in readings, I am actually shown cards in my head for that person I am reading, but that is another story. Originally, I thought that cards confused me, and I didn't need them, but the truth is I do not have that talent required to take a card's meaning and put it together with my intuitiveness so I admire anyone who can.

As time moved on in the house, I started to understand a bit more about how this all works (not nearly enough just yet). One day, while going online to try to get yet another reading, I had a chance conversation with a very experienced medium called Jan. Speaking to Jan for some time online, she directed me to a fantastic workshop for me to attend, to experience how this works and hopefully make things a bit clearer for me. I waited for that Sunday five-hour workshop to come around and had no idea what to expect, but I was excited.

On the day of the workshop, I sat at my desk on an online forum of different faces from all around the world. The host, Tony, explained that our first exercise would involve us splitting into groups of three and doing an exercise called "What are they doing now?"

As he was talking, the penny slowly dropped.

Hang on a minute, shit, I am so out of my depth! These people are all practicing mediums in a brush-

up circle. I think I've been tucked up here; now I'm going to look a complete tit!

We were broken off into groups of three, and I sat there, completely red-faced, trying to explain that "I just felt something around me. I have no idea what I'm doing here, I can't do this!"

The two ladies both laughed and told me to relax and take my time.

"What do I take my time doing though?" I asked with a big uncomfortable grin, feeling stupid.

"Take your time, use your imagination," said one of them. She continued, "My father died when he was thirty-eight. Use your imagination and tell me what you think he might be doing right now."

It took a bit of grumbling from me and hoping I would have a power cut, but eventually she convinced me to just give it a go.

"OK, well, for some reason I feel like your dad's car did not match his job. No idea why, but that's the feeling."

"Carry on," she said.

"I feel like he works in a shop, but I feel like he is overqualified to be just a shop worker; I can't explain why I feel like that at all. The car actually looks like a sandy coloured old truck, and he is throwing fishing gear in the back, by a big lake. Oh, and I see a golden retriever in the passenger seat."

"Anymore?" she asked.

"Only brown hair," I replied, feeling stupid.

She looked at me with a big grin and told me her dad was a chemist, drove a sandy coloured, beat-up old truck, had brown hair, and loved fishing! He didn't have a dog though...

She then said, "Our family dog died last week. A golden coloured Labrador. You just told me that my dog is now with my dad."

WHAT THE FUCK JUST HAPPENED? AND HOW?

I literally just sat there for a few seconds with my jaw hanging down. Until that moment, I always thought the jaw hanging down thing was something exaggerated for TV! She was emotional too so I could tell she wasn't just appeasing me; this had actually made her well up and it all made sense to her! It was far too specific to be a lucky guess, there is just no way; there were too many points and what I was saying didn't even make sense to me!

The rest of the little exercises for the day I was rubbish at. That first exercise had put me into a state of shock and I just didn't get into the others because all

I could think about was all the information in my life I must have had given to me that I just passed off as imagination. I knew this was real and had just proven it to myself. I probably got carried away in my thinking but certainly wondered how I could make more people see this. From that moment, I wanted this to be a normal accepted thing, not just something these fear mongers own and keep from the world, not when it could help so many people!

While my mind wandered, I started thinking about the times things had flashed in for no reason. Things that had got me out of trouble too. Times I had been up to no good when younger, mischief, and then a scenario popping into my head for no reason that played out. I was acting on it, getting me out of hot water and not being able to understand how I knew what was going to happen; it started making sense now!

The fact for me right then was that everything I knew about everything had just changed and I was left with no room for doubt! So, there I was, sitting shocked; all this time looking for answers from all the people I asked to help me, and this was how it worked? Could someone not have just explained it like that instead of telling me all this other bullshit that makes the whole industry a bit more mysterious? If anything, possibly it was an anti-climax, but at the same time, I know now why it is so difficult for mediums to split thoughts from messages. I later found out how to split the messages from my own thoughts. It is a lot easier than I imagined!

All I could think of now, was if I had to do something with this new way of understanding...

4.

WHAT NOW? WHY?

The days following my "training day", or whatever it was called, I tried to work out in my head what I was going to do with this newfound way of contacting Spirit.

Do I have to use it? Why me? Am I supposed to do something profound and special with my "powers"?

Obviously now I realise that this is something we all have access to, but during that time, I thought I was some sort of special chosen one! To clarify, yes, we all have access to this, but I do feel that if it is buried away, it will be no use at all until we start paying attention or Spirit decides to kick us up the arse when we are having a tough time. Something that was said to me when I asked why some can get more than others was, "Anyone can sing in the shower, but that doesn't mean we can all sell out stadiums." And no, I couldn't sell out a stadium, I'm more of a pub 'singer', if you like.

Some of us can see lots and can expand, offering the smallest of details. Some of us get the odd snippet but enough to know there is something and look deeper. Some of us have too much noise from everyday life to notice a thing. Some days I can be so tired that I get nothing at all and some days I can leave the biggest sceptic completely gobsmacked.

Imagine if everyone was aware of this. Imagine the way this world would iron out so many problems if we could go round every person and ask them just to trust this and, "Say what you see." Imagine the violence that could be prevented, the arguments that needn't happen, and the fear of death being the absolute end no longer a factor.

If one lady told me to trust what I imagine and just say what I saw her father doing, resulting in me giving such a detailed account, then why is this not talked about in this simple way? What's with the sage, prayers, and secrecy? For me, after 36 years of thinking it's all rubbish only then to find this out, tells me we must be a bit blind or closed off as a race not to have this all figured out by now. I mean dogs are psychic and we can accept that. Do they tell each other it's rubbish too or just utilise it?

The fear and scepticism we fill our minds with clearly even makes something easily demonstrated quite hard to accept. I say "easily demonstrated" because I use this a lot with clients to show how I work. I talk about someone who has passed and tell them what they imagined she looked like before they get a chance to tell me. It really is shocking how accurate this exercise is and I find it so helpful when trying to explain why things feel a bit weird to them or what's going on.

I know the three images that this lady in Spirit passes and in what order and 99% of the time can tell a client what they saw and in what order. It's quite simple when we stop burning sage for long enough to pay attention to what we are being shown! It's just a shame the theatrics sometimes drown out the clearest messages.

WE CAN ALL DO THIS! If you don't believe that, try me. Again, why is it so easy to accept that other animals have a sixth sense yet so hard to believe we do? Yes, some things don't make sense at times of readings from a genuine medium, but very often they will do eventually. I believe Spirit does this to prove that we are not just reading psychically. However, I do feel it is important to pass enough evidence that does make sense at the time in order for the bits that don't to be taken seriously enough to be noticed in the future.

A client of mine, some time ago now, who came for a reading with me was a lady called Erin. I had so much come through during this reading, but nothing made sense to her. We were both so confused and, to be honest, if I was her, I would have thought I was a useless tit. It was a car crash!

I quite rightly refunded Erin and sent her a link for another 30 minutes free of charge because I was so confused over what had happened. I mean I've had readings where nothing came through and I just had to accept I couldn't read that person for whatever reason. But with Erin there were so many energies around her that I was certain it would be good reading. When described though, she had no clue!

Erin was fantastic and she was happy to try again, so we did, and guess what—same thing! Same descriptions, same blank stares, same feeling of wanting the ground to swallow me whole.

I was so confused and genuinely felt I had let this lady down. I let it get to me and spent a few nights feeling ashamed that this trust was misplaced with me and thought back to the times when I wanted answers so badly but got nothing back. A few weeks later, we even tried again with her mother sitting in on the Zoom call also. I had the same descriptions, same blank stares but this time with her mother sitting there to make me look that bit sillier. It was clear I was getting something wrong here massively. Although there was one difference…

What I was shown was a pair of cupped hands holding a small bird, so I relayed this. Both ladies sat there saying they had no idea what that meant, but Erin wrote it down, just in case. A few days later, I had an email pop up.

"Sean, you are a class act!"

Eh? What? How?

I opened it up and there was a picture of someone I later learned was her sister, standing with her hands cupped, outside her home, with a wild bird, looking like Zorro, just sitting there in her hands! To put this into perspective, think about how long you could stand with your hands cupped before a little wild bird would come and sit there. This left me gobsmacked. More importantly, regardless of how bad the readings went, this was no fluke or psychic thing. Now, I have no idea what type of bird it was, but it was wild. Possibly a tit of some sort to represent the tit that tried to give her that reading!

This, as far as I'm concerned, was Spirit trying so hard to send Erin a message that they gave something against the odds to try to show they were there. I'm very grateful to Spirit for that, and I think a wild bird landing in someone's hands, just sitting there for a photo too, is so unlikely that if anyone tried to argue it was something else, it would be laughable, especially considering the lead-up to the event.

Erin, your patience with me was very much appreciated and I look forward to talking to you again.

Cropped to protect privacy

Back to before I was giving readings, to the time I had just started to learn how this all worked…

As the days went on, I started to talk to people close to me about what was going on. I work in engineering - commercial machinery repair, crossed with plumbing and electrics. My friends mostly work on building sites and this subject was going to be a bit odd to bring up in the pub when we next met up.

When I came to this house where it all started, I gave up my office in a business centre to save costs; after all, there was plenty of room here, so it made sense. I have two permanent staff members at my day business, one called James, an engineer, and one in the office to manage the business, her name is Emma. I had not really said a lot about what I was experiencing in this house as they might have been freaked out or think I was losing the plot, but after that training day, describing the father of the other medium in that workshop, I couldn't keep quiet about it and had to tell her and James what happened.

Emma was late for work on this particular day and we had the usual office stuff to do on a Monday that just seemed so unimportant with the events of the day before. When she got to work, I blurted it all out. "I'm a medium!" Then I told her everything that had been going on. It was hard to gauge her reaction, but it was one of those times where I say something that I wish I maybe hadn't.

After a few awkward hours of work, catching up with invoicing and sorting out the schedule for jobs that needed booking in, she asked a question.

"What do you see around me then?"

OK, good question,* I thought, *but I'm new to this. Was it just a fluke or shall I just give it a go?

I gave it a go.

That afternoon was shocking to me. The more I described, the more Spirit seemed to come forward. I realised that every "yes" from Emma to confirm that something made sense, gave Spirit that bit more trust to expand, almost like Spirit wanted to see Emma trust what I was saying or how I was interpreting what I was given before they would give me more details.

I was getting smells, words, descriptions, and feelings, at one point I could even taste tobacco. The family around her in Spirit built up such a detailed description for me that by the end of the afternoon, with all that detail, it was like a family reunion in my office! I now completely trusted. This, combined with the day before, meant there was too much evidence passed for this to be something that I could possibly have "just got lucky" with.

About a week or so later, something I found quite funny happened in the office. Something Emma didn't find funny at all at the time…

Obviously, by now, she knew I could do mediumship but wasn't aware of how often Spirits were around. I couldn't exactly say, "Oh yeah, well, my grandad and my stepmother seem to be around a lot," but I was feeling Spirit around and knew who it was. I had at this time only small bits from my dad, but was aware he was around also.

I had forgotten to call a customer back and Emma had just gotten off the phone with that angry customer after taking all the abuse for my mistake. She was already having a difficult day, but that was the final straw. At the time, although I had given a reading for her, I still thought she might think I was a bit crazy.

"Why do I have to keep dealing with customers that you keep pissing off? Every day I get moaned at by someone and you sit there with no clue what you are supposed to be doing because you're on another planet!"

And on… And on. I had been well and truly told, but I deserved it! This wasn't the time for my usual stupid remark and making light of things. I made sure she couldn't see I was trying not to laugh and sat there with a serious face, nodding. While I was sitting there, reminding myself to be serious and that now really wasn't the time for a silly joke, Emma stormed out of the room to the kitchen to put the kettle on or just get away from my stupid blank face.

While she was in the kitchen, I heard her shout out that she had been poked in the back! I instantly had a clear vision of who had done it and could feel the humour from Spirit. I explained who it was and that they were just having a laugh and were still laughing at the awkwardness of the situation, but Emma was definitely not laughing! It's important to stress that they were laughing at the awkwardness of the situation they had landed me in, not at Emma.

What happened next took every piece of determination from me not to burst out laughing. If I had laughed, I'm sure she would have left her job and not come back, but it was really hard work stopping myself during the reaction I was just about to see.

She was really shouting this time...

> "IT'S BAD ENOUGH I HAVE TO DEAL WITH YOUR SHIT, NOW I HAVE YOUR FAMILY FUCKING AROUND TOO! I JUST WANT TO DO MY JOB, SEAN; NOT CONSTANTLY SAY SORRY FOR YOUR FUCK-UPS AND PUT UP WITH THIS WEIRD SHIT NOW TOO! WHAT GIVES THEM THE RIGHT TO POKE ME IN THE BACK? TELL THEM TO LEAVE ME ALONE AND STAY OUT OF MY SPACE. IN FACT, I'LL FUCKING TELL THEM MY-SELF. WHO WAS IT?"

Her arms in the air now because she was so angry, this time addressing Spirit, still very annoyed with the situation…

> "WHOEVER THOUGHT THAT WAS FUNNY, CAN YOU PLEASE FUCK OFF AND STAY OUT OF MY SPACE? IT'S HARD ENOUGH PUTTING UP WITH SEAN'S IMMATURE CRAP WITHOUT HIS IMMATURE FAMILY ADDING TO IT!"

With that, she left to go for lunch.

Sitting there a bit shocked but still giggling about it, I realised that Spirit had played a perfect hand by removing any doubt and having a laugh at the same time.

I thanked them for being around and for what they had done. Even though I thought it was really funny, I asked them very nicely to please not do that again; as much as I had appreciated the interaction, I would really struggle to keep up with all the office work on my own so could do without Emma leaving this job thinking she was under Spirit attack or something.

Credit to Emma for not having any fear and for setting her boundaries with Spirit. There was nothing evil going on, just a bit of immature humour. Poke someone who is really mad, just to stoke the fire a bit and see me try to manage the situation while they find it all really funny, perfectly matching their characters while they were here in their human bodies. Thankfully, she does now see the funny side and I'm very grateful that I'm not stuck keeping this office running on my own.

Following on from this, over the next few weeks I still craved more information and was busy learning everything I could. Things like getting into meditating, learning about reiki (even becoming a reiki master), remote viewing, tarot cards and everything else you could imagine. To say it took over my life would be an understatement because I was hyper focussed.

Not long after the poke in the back event, I had arranged to meet four friends for a catch-up and a few beers on the Saturday coming up. It had been a while and I was looking forward to getting out and having a laugh. In fact, I had got so absorbed by all of this that I was looking forward to going out for a giggle the next day, just with my mates, away from this world. It would no doubt involve drinking too much then feeling rough the next day.

After the first few pubs, and many beers, we were sitting in a pub in my hometown. It was quieter in there and we had been chatting away for a while when my friend Andy, who could see me looking at him a bit oddly, asked what was up. The conversation was flowing so I just said it...

"Sorry mate, it's been a bit crazy. I won't go into details, but I'm fairly sure I'm a medium because lots of things have been happening and I see things around people that I always thought was just my imagination all my life."

Oh shit! Now I could tell my best friends were concerned for my mental health. I needed to show them, so I just blurted out why I was looking at him differently.

"I can see a young boy around you; he's showing me a little white dog. I have to say, mate, this boy feels like your brother."

A huge grin appeared on Andy's face.

"OK, you couldn't have known that."

He then explained that he had a brother who died very young, not long before Andy was born, and the family had a little white dog at that time also. He had never spoken about it and that was all he needed for me not to be so crazy.

Dave, sitting next to Andy, then asked me if I could see his granddad.

"Sorry, mate, not straight away, but you do have a nineteen-year-old male who was in a road accident who died hitting a tree."

His face said it all. He knew exactly who I was talking about.

Then Paul, to Dave's right-hand side, next to me on this oval table, I told him I could see a male around him, and it felt like he was in the navy. He was showing me him standing in a boxing stance with shirt sleeves rolled up. As I said it, I got more.

"He was a boxer in the navy and won a trophy boxing. A silver trophy on a wooden base is in a cupboard with a glass door and it feels like there is a bit of a gripe in the family about it. He's saying to let it go."

Paul looked at me and explained that he was supposed to inherit that trophy, but another family member had it. I don't know who it was in his family, but Paul demanded I tell him his name, or it must be bullshit.

"It doesn't work like that, mate; I didn't get his name."

"Why not?"

"I don't know, you fucking moron; did I not just give you enough evidence? I'm still working out how it works!"

Paul disappeared to the toilet for a bit, came back quiet, looking confused, and said he didn't know how I knew it but if I couldn't give a name then it was bullshit.

I had to laugh at this conversation and the fact he was so insistent I was just guessing. Paul laughed too but still looked confused. If I had found the information somewhere, I would have had the name too, surely? The only name I did get was Vera. He then explained that Vera was his grandmother. Turns out the person in Spirit showing me all this was her brother.

Chad, one of my closest friends, was sitting to my left. I didn't bother trying with Chad because as soon as I turned my head, he said he just wanted a beer and a catch-up and not to bother with him, and I respect that.

He also made it clear he thinks it's all bullshit, so he didn't even want to hear it because that's what he believes, and I respect that too, more so than him playing along and not saying how he felt about the subject just to spare my feelings. We are very close friends and it's important to respect what anyone's beliefs are if ours are respected too; as long as no one tries to ram any beliefs down anyone else's necks, anyone can get along with each other just fine. The fact that we are such close friends even now is testament to that.

I felt relieved to have it out in the open with friends and people around me because I worried about how I would be looked at by people close to me. The main concern was knowing what I knew but being perfectly aware of how I would react if someone told me this was happening to them before my awakening.

Even if someone close to you questions your mental health (in a productive way), what's the problem? Being concerned for you shows they care, so if they have in-built scepticism, of course that would be the first concern! Just accept that they care and look at it this way... Empaths are likely to have a list of earlier mental health issues anyway, so don't be too hard on them for thinking the most logical thing first.

Beliefs are just that and so long as we don't use those beliefs to mentally or physically harm others, what's the harm? There are countless religions with followers of that religion doing good things, being good people, doing no harm to others. Unfortunately, religion does seem to have a habit of creating conflict! I can't get my head around the fact that people are willing to give their lives in the name of a religion if they have had no proof of what they believe. But that is not a subject I will be talking about in this book any more than I have already done.

I am only Spiritually minded because I have had demonstrations and confirmations. I cannot follow something without proof or a very convincing explanation, let alone create conflict or imagine harming another person due to nothing more than a belief that is different from theirs!

Spirituality or some of its 'followers', however, do have issues that could do with being aired! I will be frank here as it makes me very angry to think about; I have to put this exactly how I feel it. Yes, I can be angry, it's healthy if there is good reason to be. Witnessing a good person getting hurt is an incredibly good reason if you ask me.

I am aware of people being told by tarot readers that they will die young. My mum, when she was younger, was told by a tarot reader that she would "not see old bones." I can't imagine how sick you would have to be to tell a young lady that. My mum was scared for years after, just waiting for the end. She has made old bones thankfully, but she probably won't like the way I worded that. Sorry Mum.

What do these people think they are doing? The other people I know of who have been told this are still alive and also much older. I have conducted enough readings to know that Spirits do not do things like that.

These people should be ashamed of themselves, not to mention the person who called herself a 'Spiritualist' yet left a friend of mine completely deflated and miserable just the day before I wrote this part of the book. This lady invited someone close to me to her house after joining a group of Spiritualists.

This lady put my friend in an incredibly low mood after telling her she was unlikely to have children due to her numerology numbers. Not only that, but she also told her that other issues, with other members of her family, were all brought on by themselves! Then she went on to say that my friend had no power to succeed in life due to the fact she had no number eights in her numerology! This woman's business card had pretty much every Spirit-related service on it. The fact that she had someone sit there for three hours to be slagged off, to then listen to how great she was and how talented, while at the same time not offering ONE piece of evidence to validate anything she was saying, made me furious.

This lady took numerology numbers, twisted them, and passed them in a negative light. Why would you do that to someone? It is people with this mindset that add to the mental health problems that are so rife with awakenings and another reason for writing this book, demonstrated perfectly, yet again, only yesterday! It makes me so sad to see something so good ruined by unhealthy Ego.

Firstly, who does this woman think she is by taking someone else's energy like that to see them leave a meeting deflated and empty? No one has the right to tell another person they have no hope of being happy because of a few numbers. Spirit offers guidance and empowerment, sometimes the odd reminder to change a behaviour but for the greater good of you and those around you. Any Spirit worker that says anything to deflate you by taking anything away from what you can do with your future is working with nothing but Ego, not Spirit.

Now, don't get me wrong; I am not saying you will leave every reading full of the joys of spring. For example, if you are in a relationship that Spirit can see is holding you back, or worse, then that may come through. The biggest difference is Spirit empowering you and trying to show you something that is no good for you because they are there for you and WANTING happiness for your future! They're certainly not drawing a line under your future happiness, because we can't tell the future. We can see a path, not a definite outcome. Giving a client information that can help them decide whether to change path is about as far as fortune-telling goes as far as I'm concerned. As I said earlier in this book, until I am channelled the winning lottery numbers that is what I'm sticking with.

If anything above is not agreeable to you for whatever reason, I need you to have a good think about it. Have a good think about why Spirit would be around you for your whole life wanting you to be happy and succeed and then tell some egocentric 'Spiritualist' to tell you there is no hope to be had. This is a disgusting way to behave and someone like this, if they carry on in that way, WILL cause someone to take their own life, if that is not already the case.

For some reason, this lady also had a swipe at fees. Something about charging more than nominal token amounts to conduct Spirit work. This is the most tiring, draining, emotionally charged thing I have ever done in my whole life, and I do this to try to help people not get sucked under by people like that. I should imagine she was happy not charging because she was not using her energy to channel. What it is clear to me is that she was draining my friend's energy and making herself feel better.

There is simply no way I can do this for free and I have never once held a gun to anyone's head to book a session with me.

Anyway, where was I?

As time went on, I continued trying to take in more information. I even spoke to more online mediums and psychics, but as I was learning and feeling more, I was becoming angrier with the ones I could see right through, the bullshitters and chancers. What was more dangerous than the blatant frauds were the ones that could connect but added and tried to expand or "fill the gaps" if you like. In all honesty, it was like some could wrap a reading up in five minutes, so they needed to fill the extra time with chuff.

This, I will say again, can be extremely dangerous. To give an example of what I am talking about I will use a recent reading that I gave to a client: The client came to me for a reading and wanted to know what her husband was up to while she was working away. Even just before the reading, he had apparently been short with her, like he was trying to get her off the phone. This was a psychic reading, so I did my visualisations as she talked about her husband and how he was trying to get her off the phone so quickly.

"Does this man have a red truck?" I asked.

"Yes," was her reply

"OK. And does your kitchen have blue tiles and a corded phone (like from the nineties) on the wall by the fridge?"

"Yes," again was her reply. Well, this was the right connection as far as I was concerned.

"OK, well, with his emotions, I can feel he seems very away with the fairies, like he is not in the room when you are talking to him. But this feels like work stress distracting him, nothing more. I think he is a mechanic who works for himself and seems stressed to you at the moment?"

"YES! Wow!"

OK, well, now we know we have the right person I can try to look to see what he's up to now.

"There is a blonde lady in the house at the moment; shorter hair, wavy like it is worn up. It seems a bit heated there like she is moaning, and he is standing, looking in the fridge for far too long, almost hoping she will go away before he turns back around."

I am not fond of these types of readings. I don't know who this lady is and why she is with her husband while his wife is away. What is important is that I only give the facts, and quite often I explain that I'm just an idiot sitting here saying what I see, take it, or leave it. Most important is to give evidence; what he drives, his job, tile colour in the kitchen, any little details like this are essential!

What would have been dangerous, and something I have seen, is to expand on the basic facts and give my own conclusion. I had what I saw, and that was it, no reason to expand at all. Saying the obvious add-on, something like, "This man is no good for you," or some crap like that to make myself look wiser or have a solution on hand is not something I have any right to do, ESPECIALLY after giving evidence and gaining trust.

Had I offered no evidence of a connection and just said he was cheating, my client would have had room for doubt, so not as bad in my opinion. But giving evidence to gain such trust and then making the rest up is dangerous. Unfortunately, I have seen it so many times and it is scary to think what could come of that sort of thing.

The client obviously asked who this lady was and why she was there, but I was running out of answers, and I could not just make it up. Sometimes I just could not get the answers; that's how it is… "I will email if anything else pops in after the reading as sometimes it does take longer than this half-hour, and the pressure of running out of time is not help-ing." It was my last reading of the day and I decided to put my feet up for half an hour to chill out, just me, a nice cold beer and silence. It was just then that, out of nowhere, I had to send a quick message; I'd had a bit more pop in and felt it was unfair not to add it.

"I do feel like this lady has a dog outside in her car. It's very odd too because I was just shown a white car parked on your drive at an angle, almost just dumped there."

"Oh, that's his mum! She can't park, and her white car is always half on the lawn at an angle, plus she matches that description. I was getting carried away and didn't even think of her," was her reply. Lucky, she didn't trust her gut with that one! See how confusing it can be? Mystery solved and no damage done.

He was distant with her on the phone because his mum was there, moaning at him about something that was probably silly compared to his work stress. As far as I am concerned, that's how it should be done—no extras, no gap-filling, no playing with people's lives.

Back to the search for more answers…

As time went on with the "hunt for information", I honestly felt like I hit a certain saturation point. The more I asked about this subject the angrier I felt myself getting with it. More fear, more scams, more to question. Even after all the evidence I had given myself, some of these people still managed to bring me back to ask myself, "Am I just crazy?"

The more I questioned and took the information in the more I felt like walking away and drawing a line under it all. Why did my search for answers carry so much in the way of telling me what to be fearful of?

Why did nearly every reading I went for involve me getting told I was to sage my house and cast negative Spirits away when I felt perfectly happy and comfortable in that place or the fact that I needed to be careful? Be careful of what? You already said I had lots of Spirit around me and had done my whole life.

Then you have the blatantly obvious scams…

"*How lucky I met you just in time to remove this awful bad luck cloud that only you have the skills to remove!"*

I had entered my email address in all sorts of websites and had a plethora of 'psychics' emailing me daily telling me my luck was about to take a turn for the better. BUT I needed their help before the window of opportunity closed because once this cloud was gone, I would be drowning in abundance. Rich beyond my wildest dreams!

People buy this shit when they are desperate and worn down. What made it worse and even more dangerous was the fact that the openings to the emails were full of information about me. Information that, to be fair, was accurate…

HOW? I do not know enough about astrology to give my opinion on the subject, but I know that I have had enough detailed information given to me by only giving my date of birth to know that this is an art! In fact, the amount that can be told about me by just giving my date of birth to the right person is scary!

What is also scary is the fact that anyone who has your date of birth can put that into a good astrology website and get enough information about your character, 99% of the time, to get you to pay attention. Now, take that detailed information about your character, add a story about being down on your luck and a few emails saying how bright your future looks, and all you need to do is remove this bad karma or dark cloud or whatever they want to call it.

You then have desperate people handing over a lot of money to scam artists that are preying on people at their lowest thinking this 'medium' will bring you good luck if only you pay the $250 before it's too late and the window of fate closes, leaving you in the shadow of bla bla bla, here we go again!

I always wondered why my date of birth was needed when I went for a reading. A genuine medium will not need that information to be able to connect and it stinks of searching for as much help as they can get to appear genuine. Possibly with the exception of confirming the sitter is old enough to be receiving a reading.

In fact, I go into a mediumship reading wanting as little information as possible about my client because any information I have can sometimes start to turn what's coming through into a sort of "soup", a blend of mediumship confused with what I already know—not helpful! Often, a client coming to me for a reading can be blown away with what is said, and sometimes this will make them want to come back soon after.

I sometimes think they are slightly disappointed the second time because that reading will never be as detailed as the one I gave when I had no preconceptions and knew nothing about them. The exceptions to this are when there is further passing or a change in circumstance that leaves questions to be answered, but hopefully you get my point with this.

Back to my original point…

As I said, a 'Psychic Medium' asking for a date of birth is a red flag, unless for age verification purposes. BUT… Giving your date of birth to a psychic who is also a skilled astrologer is different!

I had an amazing reading given to me by a lady in the USA using my date of birth. She even wanted to know what time I was born on my birthday to help her understand where my position was on a birth chart. I did not know the exact birth time, but she was so skilled that, just by using my character, she told me what time I was born that day! What?

I later confirmed this with my mum as she looked through old boxes and told me, "Yes, this woman told you what time you were born to the minute! It was so precise and detailed! Everything she said she picked up from these charts, also incorporating tarot, was mind-blowing based on my time and date of birth! I take my hat off to her and would recommend her to anyone. What was the difference? She was skilful and responsible and presented everything she was saying in detail and explained why she was saying it. This is an art that clearly takes a huge amount of time to master, and I was extremely impressed.

My next point is something I feel is especially important and something that can be easily done in a psychic reading, leading to misinformation.

My kids like playing a game that involves connecting psychically and telling me what number I have written down and they are shamefully good at it! I'll write a number down between 1 and 100; they then sit, focus, and try to get the number that I have. They text me when they are ready, to save the other sibling from hearing if they just shouted the number out. It's amazing how well they both do; I'm talking 70–75% accuracy. That is like "Operation Stargate" type accuracy from these two kids and I am enormously proud of them!

If you are wondering, Operation Stargate was a US government program set up to evaluate the viability of using remote viewing within the military, a remarkably interesting subject to read about. Apparently, no Psychics are used now, and the details were declassified.

I tried an exercise to see if I could fool my kids and demonstrate how a psychic reading can be wrong sometimes. I got my sheet of paper and wrote down the number three. While I had the number three on the piece of paper, I concentrated hard on the number nine. The same way you would concentrate on a situation you may be suspicious of if you were to see a psychic to ask if your boyfriend was cheating, for example. *(Page number entirely coincidental!)*

We cannot help but build a worst-case scenario in our heads; why else would we be asking a psychic for answers to such a question if there was no suspicion or scenario we had imagined? The number nine in my head was my worst-case scenario when the fact/situation was the number three, written in black and white. My kids were both focused and, after a while, I had both text messages in...

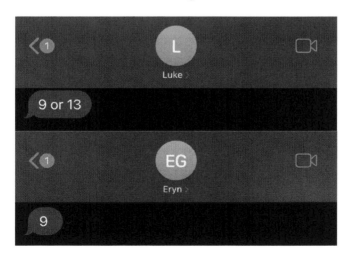

The situation in my head was so vivid that they read that as a fact, not what was written down. They read my energy, missing the 'fact'.

This exercise, so brilliantly demonstrated by my kids, says to me this: If you go to a psychic reading with such a vivid suspicion built up, you will sometimes channel that and cloud out the fact like a big beacon of doubt. I had to investigate this more, and, yes, after going for a couple of readings to assess this theory, it was very much the case.

Now, this is not the fault of a psychic that is genuine, after all, my kids try very hard to do well at this game, and they do if the conditions are correct, but I do think we should at least be aware of this being a possibility so that we do not make any drastic life changes because of what we are told when our heads are full of suspicion. Psychic or remote viewing is something that has been scientifically proven. Mediumship is something that scientists still question, but I see that changing in the extremely near future.

I highly recommend completely clearing your head of any expectation or will for a specific answer should you sit for a reading because if your head is noisy during a psychic or energy reading, it definitely can play a part in the reading, clouding out what may be the real facts.

So here I was giving readings, offering evidence and frankly, feeling like I was doing a good thing whenever I passed something to someone because the way they reacted, told me it was a help to them.

Maybe I should think about doing this professionally...

SEAN GRAHAM

5.

BECOMING A PAID MEDIUM

It's around three months now since the first work-shop and me getting on with life and work while spending my spare time still reading about so many different points of view; I call them points of view because I find nothing harder than reading a book about Spirituality with someone giving instructions as if they have the rule book. You must say this prayer; you MUST do this or that; you must use the symbols I receive from Spirit as a basis for your learning...

Well, I don't agree with that. How can it be the same for everyone? One circle I found was run by a man called Julian with the help of Elena, both fantastic mediums. This was a group I felt more comfortable in, and there did not seem to be the unhealthy Ego or power trip that was in other groups I had tried. I felt more comfortable there with the way I looked at things as opposed to having to be silent with my views, knowing I would be told I was wrong. This was my new circle now and I felt welcome. Thank you both. I still struggle in a group setting though, and it's something I am working on. I still can't handle the fact I can give readings and be confident but when it comes to a group, my head just tells me over and over again how many people will see me fuck up, then I do! Luckily, I have no plans to do platform demonstrations in the near future.

It was funny how much I realised after joining this group, how Egotistical some other circles are and although I believe Healthy Ego is a thing we need, an unhealthy Ego is very off-putting for someone trying to learn more and be confident enough to progress. Elena helped me understand this.

I know we get told to remove the Ego a lot and, yes, I can fully understand how that gets in the way; I agree. BUT! I personally believe that while we are in these bodies with any form of day-to-day life, there will always be an element of Ego with everything we do. I feel it's important to be aware of what our Ego is and where our Ego gets in the way; that is for sure! We need to understand the difference between healthy Ego and unhealthy Ego rather than just try to be totally Ego free.

If I get bad feedback, it hurts my Ego. If someone says something bad about me, it hurts my Ego. I have tried but cannot remove it so I will just be AWARE of it. Sometimes, when looking so hard to make a connection, we get so hung up on the list of things we have to do that while we are doing all these things, we miss the small bits and overpressure ourselves. I can only speak for myself, but the pressure of 'what I was supposed to be doing', if anything, slowed me down.

I was at my day job the other day and needed to pop to a site to sort an electrical issue out for a customer that runs a hotel. The whole place was empty apart from the owner, James. He is well aware of my work as a medium and he mentioned to me that he was alone in the building about a week before and felt like someone was looking through the door from the restaurant area to the kitchen. Incidentally, in the last chapter, I talk about James' brother, Tom and the event that happened with him, something that shocked me!

As he talked, I felt a male by that window and had a picture start to build up. I said I felt he wore one of the jackets that can be a bit stinky, the wax jackets that are hard to wash. And he had very deep wrinkles on his face (weathered) a bit like Phil Tufnell. I could feel a hat and he looked almost like a bookmaker, leading me to suspect a connection to horses.

The owner told me it sounded like I was describing the previous property owner, a man who had horses, and when he looked up a picture on his phone from an old article about the place on the internet, there he was, looking like Phil Tufnell in a wax jacket. He was just popping by to see the place. Not a trapped soul that needs to walk towards the light or any of that; just saying hello because it was a huge part of his life.

My view is that for the current owner to feel something and me to be able to give some sort of connection with what I was feeling, for me, that backs up my point about everyone being able to do this but they're not aware, until they are aware, but fear and scepticism creep in to tell us that this is ridiculous.

So here we have an obviously tuned-in man saying he felt something, but then thinking "nah, it can't be" and passing it off. We all have Spirit around us, but sometimes Spirit pushes harder, or we simply have quiet that we did not have before, making some, more tuned in or "wake up". The situation made me wonder what he would make of it all if he tried to strengthen his connection by going online and learning what he could, maybe from other Spirit workers in readings or whatever he can find to read up on.

The problem is, the signs and feelings that made us start looking into all this a bit deeper can soon be drowned out by individuals telling us to use protection prayers, join a Spiritual church, buy a load of crystals, learn tarot, get a crystal ball, assume every-one around you is a narcissist and write down all your dreams! Why not just one step at a time?

You take an everyday person who is "normal" and, yes, he can be open to the idea of Spirit and get his head around it. So then this "normal" man who is getting his head around it and starting to believe or, more importantly, TRUST that feeling can now think, *Although it's a bit crazy I know this is a thing,* so he then starts trying to contact Spirit work-ers for confirmation or a bit of guidance.

Once we dive into what at times is so fucking egotis-tical it's ridiculous, we are thrown so much other crap and fear to think about, that one of two things hap-pen:

We convince him he was having a breakdown and there's no way he can carry on going down that path after hearing all the other crazy shit he has just been told...

Or he starts delving too deep, takes rules as gospel because he is keen for information and trusts what he is told by everyone because "Yeah, it sounds crazy but so was being able to feel a dead man around me so everything must be true after all, even what this crazy bastard is telling me with no evidence offered."

I witness this too often and it's sad to see. Truths and rumours all mixed up until, one day, a normal man turns up for work stinking of burnt sage, rattling and bent double with all the crystals hanging off him. Also, now his 'boundaries' are so in check that he has pushed away everyone who doesn't totally agree with all his new "rules" that he has just learned; insistent on stating these rules as fact because they were told to him by the same person that told him how gifted he was, so they must know what they are talking about.

This is obviously an exaggeration, but hopefully you can see what I am saying. And no, James is not like that at all; it was just a hypothetical scenario but one I very nearly found myself in.

It's not easy to admit but all these readings I was going for, getting repeatedly told how "gifted" I was, nearly turned me into a very Egotistical arsehole, or at least worse than I already am! I am just grateful that my argumentative side kicked in when it did to allow me to question everything a bit more.

It didn't take long to consider that just because it was a nice thing being said about me and my "gifts", it was just the same bullshit as the other stuff I was told. It felt like the whole industry was either misled or just full of shit. It was thoughts like this that made me one night just think, *FUCK IT!*

"I'm going to be a paid medium too, and I will be the most honest, basic, say-what-I-see medium I can be. I want to make this more normal for people, with no fancy crap that 'normal' people would be scared off by. This industry is its own downfall and it's a shame it is so full of shit, leaving sceptics to remain sceptic, missing some very special things that could happen in their lives just because the theatrical crap has scared them off."

I nearly was, and I know what my mental state was like at the time, so if I can help anyone connect and cope better, that's what I will do. The only problem I had was how do I structure a reading? Who do I think I am, thinking I know what to do as far as giving readings is concerned? Every reading I had given was as simple as saying how I worked and then telling them what I was picking up on. Readings I had been to, had always been a lot more polished or detailed.

But was I looking for anything more than just the basics? All I was ever looking for was some evidence that showed me this is real, something to be said that the reader had no way of knowing. Either proof they were psychic or proof I had Spirit around me.

With everything you have read in previous chapters, you will be aware that I have had my eyes opened by individuals who have taught me valuable lessons to enable me to do this. At this time, I think I forgot this and took the narrative that every truth I had heard could have been blended with lies and decided that I didn't trust anything I had been told in this 'industry' unless I had witnessed it myself.

I stress that it's only a SMALL NUMBER of workers in this industry that ruin it for others. There are so many fantastic Spirit workers I have met that are doing fantastic things for the right reasons and helping countless people for the better. The problem is the best mediums are usually harder to find. The most detailed readings I have ever had are by individuals that I would struggle so hard to find online and have only met by chance. Probably, because like myself, they only have a smaller local ad online and not a big worldwide google budget.

I decided on the name of my Spirit page…

"Sean - No BS - Psychic Medium."

A completely no-frills psychic medium. Say what I see; try to give evidence, and nothing more. I set my listings up and waited to see what happened.

I had already been offering trust readings locally, putting my number online for people to call for a reading, only having to pay if I could blow their socks off. This was new though and seemed to move faster.

I had the idea of offering a picture reading; you send me a picture and I will send you back what I see when

I focus and ask Spirit to give me something. Just a free sentence and, that way, you can take or leave my service. Completely pressure-free and no way I could feel like I was pressuring or ripping anyone off. If anything, I overstated how basic I was as my biggest fear was being seen as someone who was just making it up. My whole reason for doing this was to help someone who was in my position, desperate to know one way or another whether they were crazy or not.

After about a day, I had my first booking. Now, this man had booked me without even taking up my offer of a free photo reading first. That with the fact I that had no reviews was a lot of trust to put into me, so it was a nice feeling.

I arranged a Zoom reading with him on the message screen, but, for some reason, when he messaged me back and said he was available that night, just the words "Yes, tonight at 7 p.m. will be great thanks," everything hit me. His pain was mine now, GRIEF! I couldn't hold it together because I was now picking up that his mother had died very recently, and he was hurting. But I was in tears! With that, I sent a message just asking if we could do the next day instead and he was happy to, thankfully, because I needed to get my shit together! Even with all the grounding and cord cutting stuff, sometimes a situation will just hit me hard, and I end up emotional.

As the Zoom call connected the next day to this male in Scotland whom I felt I suddenly knew so well, it seemed to just all to come out. I had no set plan, but I explained to him how I get messages and even the true reason why I had to postpone. "You've just lost your mum, haven't you?"

He looked at me and nodded. Not a huge amount came through as evidence that day, but she was referring to his dad, showing me an image of him hammering wood on a roof. Turns out he is a carpenter.

You see I don't think it's always like we see on the TV when you get a theatrical story, and everything makes perfect sense! Sometimes yes, you do, but I'd love to see the editing process of these shows as I refund around 8–10% of readings purely because I can't get much, and it won't provide any value. I know the argument is that I'm still using energy so I shouldn't refund, but I'm never going to be able to do that. Evidence of some sort that is unquestionable or your money back.

So here we were, me talking to a total stranger and feeling instantly his pain. Yes, I only got one other piece of evidence surrounding his father's career, but two pieces of valid evidence, to me, is better than 20 bits of vagueness.

I found myself explaining how I see it working when we pass over, in my usual black-and-white way of looking at things, and it goes something like this: When we "die" or cross or pass or whatever we are calling it today, I have a theory that I can best describe as the "what the fuck?" moment.

I still say die, but you know what I mean, and, yes, I am aware we never actually die, but you get a DEATH certificate, and I feel no guilt using that word because we are still humans in a human society.

What I mean by the "what the fuck?" moment is what I can only imagine from my point of view…

I have had Spirit confirm this to some extent; even my dad in Spirit when he finally came through gave me a confirmation of this.

I know we expect a couple of angels waiting for us when we die and we know exactly what's happening, get whisked onto an elevator to the pearly gates to ride a white unicorn along a cloud to meet up with family; but let's take the fairy tale out of all this for a moment and think rationally. All we have is Spirit contact and people's accounts of near-death experiences. Some conflict my opinions, some back them up.

Imagine you die…

I imagine that there is an initial period of time, just after passing, when you are just thinking, *What the fuck?* I think we have a lot to learn when we pass before we can be a master communicator with another dimension, no different to us here learning to contact

Spirit.

A bit like when you fly abroad on holiday…

You might have to call your mum when you land to say you got there safe, but the signal is bad, you are two bus journeys from the hotel, and not familiar with where to even catch the first bus. Your tour guide is all smiles and welcomes but not actually helping you with much information yet. So, you make a crackly call with what signal you do get, but it cuts out and you really need to get moving to get that bus, so you'll have to talk later when you get there, but at least it was something if you did manage to get through, even if it was patchy.

Now, the bus journey to the hotel, as in my example, as far as I see it, is the learning to pass messages. We presume that it's all going to be perfect as soon as we pass over and I can say from my experience of the family I have in Spirit that it's the ones that died long ago that give me the most detail.

Some pass and are extremely present as soon as they cross over! I suppose their hotel was at the airport with a big free to use phone, ready to make clear contact but who knows the finer details, all we know is that it can take time.

I used to get a couple of words from my dad. You know when you talk to yourself in your head, like that but different, like it's clear as day and their voice is accompanied by the words on a road sign. I wanted so much to hear from my dad clearly, but all I could ever get was, "SEAN, IT'S YOUR DAD," nothing more. He used to say that when he phoned me like I didn't know who it would be. Something silly always made me smile and then I could say something sarcastic back about being glad he told me in case I thought it was my nan or something stupid like that.

My dad died in 2017 and, other than the couple of words, I got nothing up until 2021. Four years to make a good connection. Now he is much easier to connect with and even typing this I felt him draw closer to have a look and smile about "SEAN, IT'S YOUR DAD."

I know that because all the hairs on my right-hand side stood up on end (my blood relative side) like you get with goosebumps. Then I could smell the baggy old woolly jumper that he used to wear when he was cleaning the cellar in the pub he ran. Some folks pass away and give fantastic evidence almost instantly. Some folks pass away and take longer to learn.

There is also a theory that we need time and Spirit will come through when the sitter is ready to receive. Now I am fully open to that, but I feel, if anything, it is certainly a combination of the two.

Back to the male I was reading for in Scotland...

He told me he was grateful for my help and that it

had certainly helped to get anything as there was no way I knew him or what I said. He then left lovely feedback for me that, quite honestly, I was very proud to receive. This rough-edged Lutonion had helped a total stranger and had passed not a lot, but enough to help.

As the days went on and more pictures turned up in my messages, I was getting booked up more and more. The feedback was also building up and reading them, quite honestly, made me emotional. I wanted to help, and I could see I was.

Things were so much better than I expected them to be. I was busy, I was helping, and I felt good knowing people were leaving my readings feeling better about things without me having to bullshit or dress anything up at all. Not everyone felt I was a help though!

Some people sat there not making sense of anything and some sat with pads and pencils asking for specific dates like "When will I have my babies? Months and years please," and, "What year will I get married?" Sometimes I explained that it would be irresponsible to give information like that as I would be making it up and fortune-telling is a very grey area because freedom will always dictate what happens ultimately.

These disappointments shouldn't have gotten to me but ultimately they did, because I didn't want to let anyone down at all, even though I don't feel that

Spirits are an answer bank; it's not their job. The Spirits' job is to show they are there for you more than anything else and that death is not final in my opinion, bring forward some memories, and acknowledge current goings on too. Yes, a Spirit can show a situation or highlight things like a relationship that they can see is hurting you, but they're not here tell you that the baby is coming in three years from now on March the 7th at 3.45 p.m.!

The way I like to explain fortune-telling is like this:

Let's say I dig a big hole outside your front door, then put a mat over it or cover it up so it somehow looks normal when you leave. You could be in your house, sitting down to get a reading, and you may get told that your future involves falling down a hole.

It's more than likely that will happen, and you'll have no idea what the reason for being told this is. After your reading you get ready to leave the house, walk out the front door and fall into a hole! Yes, the fortune teller was correct; you fell into a hole ... congratulations! The thing is the hole was already there; you just weren't aware of it.

So yes, we can tell the future if the path is already laid out for us, but I don't believe we can interfere with free will and other people's choices enough to give specific details in the future. How boring would life be if we could not alter an event that might or might not take place? I may be wrong, but as I said before, every psychic would have won the lottery by now if it were that accurate.

The readings kept piling in and I was pre-booked for several months ahead at one point. It was an amazing feeling seeing people's faces when I passed something, and they said how happy it made them to be given evidence that was so undeniable.

The feedback built up and the reviews said how amazing the readings were. I noticed that this went from something I could do easily, with no pressure, to suddenly having a reputation to uphold. And this was something that my head wanted to play with. "Let's mess with Sean's head and remind him constantly how much pressure this feedback has put him under." You see, without the feedback the client had no expectations, but the more feedback that was left the more disappointed I would be if I just couldn't read someone, and it hurt me more than I was aware. It hurt because I've felt that disappointment and my Ego told me I'd be able to help everyone.

That help is valuable, and if I can't help I'm a failure. It's valuable because, at that moment, knowing I could not have known what I passed them, the doubt and worry about a loved one being gone forever and ceasing to exist was gone.

Generally, when I did a batch of readings, I had five or six to get through as any more than that was exhausting to the point that it wasn't even worth me trying. What made it exhausting was this… And please understand that if you do this yourself, it is no fault of yours, just the way my brain works.

If the client didn't want to engage with me at all, I could feel it. The words "general" or "blind" reading just told me it would be hard work. Like my mind just presumed this was some sort of test because when I said blind reading in the past, it was never just a blind reading. I knew what I wanted to hear; I just didn't talk about the subject that I wanted to cover in the hope the medium would just know.

So often have I given readings, passing all sorts of information, validated information that was helpful, and then right at the end of the reading, the client will say something like, "I was really hoping my sister would have come through."

Almost like clockwork, when I hear something like that at the end of a reading, I get a piece of evidence, a description, or something that says the person is there. I will always say to the client something like, "Were they a quiet or shy person?" Most of the time I will be told yes. While they were here, if they weren't the sort of person who would barge into a conversation without being asked, the same would likely happen in readings.

One example that stands out for me is a lady I was talking to one day who told me right at the end of the reading that she really wished her aunt would have come through. As soon as she uttered those words, I got a lady with curly blonde hair, and more relevant was what came through next...

"Did she have a dog called Charlie?"

"Oh my God, yes!"

"Well, she is here but clearly didn't want to interrupt."

I know the way we are looked at, but I can state from the bottom of my heart that I do not want people to talk to me to try to dig out facts or cold read. That goes for many other readers who do this for the right reasons. Unfortunately, these charlatans that plague this good thing make us look bad at times and understandably cause this feeling of having to say, "General reading," and sit there saying nothing.

Spirit likes to be part of the conversation, and this is where the best evidence comes through. Remember in the first chapter where the sitter's father corrected what she told me about how many toolboxes he had? Now, if that lady had sat there with her arms folded just saying yes and no, that would never have happened. I promise you; this is so common and so frustrating but in no way the fault of a sitter!

My mum once told her friend to come for a reading with me, and she said to him not to give me anything, just yes and no and see what I get. She was subconsciously saying, "Careful he doesn't cold read you!"

Thanks, Mum, put him on the defensive before we even talk!

Now, when he called, I had a blood relative of his trying to come through and the feeling or need to talk about a sister, so I asked straight away. I know I should have asked Spirit for more, but I was talking to a family friend so didn't feel the need to do too much in the way of a show. After all, I would be able to pass far more detailed evidence at some point anyway, so to save the time getting the basics and spend the time more wisely this was what I asked.

My exact words were, "Why am I being told to ask about a sister?" Now I knew this was a blood relative, and although I was feeling the sister question, I had not yet made the link. As we were so early into the call, it was just that and a need to ask about a sister.

He said the words, "I don't know," so I moved on and asked Spirit to give me more details so I could pass something valuable. Surely if there was a reason to ask that, he would have said, so I just ignored everything else around that. He only spoke to say yes or no, and I knew I was struggling with someone who clearly didn't want to talk to me. Then all I could think was,

What is the deal with this? Why's he being so grumpy?

Other images that had built up while I was asking about a sister were totally ignored as he said he didn't know, so I moved on.

When I later asked my mum what the deal was with him, she said that she told him to say nothing at all! I said how hard it was talking to someone who clearly didn't want to talk and the way it makes your mind just shut off. The time spent bringing forward information was instead spent thinking, **What the hell is up with him?**

Sometimes, Spirits are very keen to step right in and the sitter will not have to say a word. But if that person was quiet or shy, then the lack of engagement will hardly make them want to pop in and say hi.

Have you ever seen an awkward conversation between two people and wanted to go over to make small talk? I certainly haven't!

Mum then told me he had lost his sister years ago and had hoped she would come forward! The other images I started to get as I asked were, by the way, an accurate description of her but the "standoffishness" wasn't really the most inviting environment for Spirit to step further forward.

The way I see it is this…

You go to see someone who hopefully will bring family members through. As our energies blend, Spirit sees an element of trust and will step forward with evidence.

Every "yes" given by the client, in response to some evidence given, and that loved one will step forward more and more, making the reading much more valuable. Add a shy or quiet character and it is slower to get evidence. Maybe they even did something that could hold an element of shame and cause them to wait until they are asked. Whatever the reasons are, if I have a standoffish client or one who is unwilling to say why they came for a reading, it will be much harder!

If I felt like I was being tested or judged, my head would just shut off and that reading would not only be completely exhausting, but it would also make me low because all I did was prove the cynic right this time when what I wanted to do all along was help.

That was until I met L! (Name protected for privacy). I had a Zoom reading booked, and when we connected, I could just tell that L wasn't expecting much from me. She then asked how I worked as she was familiar with the process and wanted to know if I was genuine. She told me she had one family member in Spirit she wanted to hear from and one current issue she wanted to investigate. In my head, all I could think was,

She thinks you're a fraud. This is going to be a disaster!

She was busting my balls mentally but wasn't aware of it. In fact, I was doing that myself, but I just thought she wanted me to mess up. Why? Because she had a strong character and I was slightly intimidated if I am completely honest. I just knew she would not go easy if I messed anything up.

A good trait to have and certainly my issue, not hers.

This was one of these readings that I would have in the past just refunded! However, I had a bit of a bad day beforehand so this day was different and I was feeling a bit pissed off anyway. Because I was a bit stressed earlier in the day and maybe had less patience, I just thought to myself, (sorry L) ***Fuck this, I'm no fraud!***

I just said what I saw instead of letting my mind get the better of me just because I thought I was being judged. L and I have spoken about this since because it stands out with me as one of those readings where I learned something and understood that, although I can't help it all the time, it's me who messes up a reading.

Had I not had a bad day, leading to a "fuck this!" mentality (ironic already because those days normally are the worst when it comes to giving readings) I would not have seen what Spirit wanted to pass and the reading would have been over before it started. It would have been such a shame if that were to be the case as what came through was valuable. The funny thing is I had just made the worst of it due to the fact I had a bad day earlier and she didn't presume I was a fraud at all, she was just trying to find out how I work.

Without going into too many details, everything I passed was correct and made sense. That includes the family member who also came through with very important advice. We have sat a couple of times since and I often say how grateful I was for that day because it made me learn that my preconceptions and fear of being judged can make a reading fall flat on its arse!

Thank you, L!

As the weeks and months went by, I started to feel like I needed a holiday. As much as I love giving readings and talking to people all over the world, something was just off now. This feeling, followed by two other events, started a "butterfly effect" if you like.

One of the scariest things that happened to me since all of this began happened out of the blue in the spring. It was really hot and my front door was very slightly ajar to try to get some air in. I was sat, ready for the first reading of the day/evening, and everything was normal. Just as I opened Zoom to connect, I looked to my right and a black cat was sitting there, in my front room staring at me, my dog asleep about one meter away.

Now, the best way to say this is that my dog, a cocker spaniel that hates cats, it would have been carnage had he noticed, and he notices everything. I can't move my head without his eye opening, so the fact that he hadn't seen this cat was strange enough. I sat still not knowing what to do but decided to dive at the dog. I grabbed him in mid-air because my moving startled him; he saw the cat and leaped at it. The cat swiftly left the house, and my dog Eric was back on his bed probably thinking about the liberty that had just been taken in his domain.

I was 10 minutes late for the reading by the time I had settled Eric and composed myself, but thankfully the client, a lady called Jessica, was very understanding when I explained why. About five minutes into this reading, I had a huge shooting pain across my chest; then my jaw tightened, and although I tried to brave through it, I was panicking. Panicking enough to dial 999 on my phone and keep my finger hovering above the call button because this felt very fucking serious!

I genuinely thought I was having a heart attack but still I tried to hide that from Jessica because I was already late, and this was just unprofessional! I was desperately hoping that if this was a heart attack, I could get through the half hour reading before getting in too much trouble to call an ambulance.

Extreme people pleasing at its best/worst!

One thing I do want to note is that Jessica also said she felt fine before connecting until we spoke and as soon as the Zoom connected her heart rate increased. We all have reactions to things that may have more meaning and this, I feel this was a very clear demonstration of feeling someone else's energy.

As fast as the pain came on, it went... I carried on the reading and explained to the client that I was really struggling and had no idea why but thanked her for her patience. Although completely baffled by the whole thing, I carried on the rest of the evening's readings. Thankfully they were not as painful.

A couple of days later, I received a message from the client that shook me slightly...

This was the message...

"I apologize for the late message, just I wanted to reach out to let you know that I discovered the reason for the black cat and the heart attack episode you had during my reading. I learned the next day that a close family friend had died the afternoon before of a heart attack (during the reading). I believe you felt her leave the physical world and enter the Spiritual. Being in touch with Spirit is an incredible gift, but I'm sure at times it can be very draining; and this is definitely one of those times. That being said, I want to thank you again for what you do. I know there are times when it can't be easy but being a portal for people to connect with their loved ones is an honourable profession and it does not go unappreciated. Thank you for the clarity you gave me, my family, and so many others.

Jessica"

My first thought was for the poor family friend and Jessica having to receive such bad news. It certainly explained the events for me, but my next thought was, *Why did I feel the pain so vividly at the time?* Surely this couldn't have been dangerous for me, could it? As I tried to get my head around this, I came to the following conclusion...

The poor lady who passed away would have been so scared, and at the time of passing over, I'm sure her reaction would be to grab and try to pull herself back. Now, this is a very basic view, but will we ever know the actual details of the process until the time comes? I imagine it's the same sort of scenario that a drowning swimmer would go through. Someone trying to help that swimmer who is in trouble, or even just someone close to that swimmer, could, in panic, be pulled under the water. Not through bad intention but through nothing more than sheer terror and panic.

I understand I was not trying to rescue someone drowning and wasn't even aware of that situation, but if "my light was on" and that was one grasp in this panic due to the fact I was talking to a family friend then I can see this as a plausible answer. That or just empathy in overdrive on this occasion, but whatever it was, it was somewhat worrying. Thankfully, I can't see this being an event that will occur very often.

We are all part of this universe, and the energy is

linked. It's shocking and frightening to think that someone having a heart attack on the other side of the world could cause me to feel such pain when I was not even aware of the situation.

I do not think for one minute that this would have killed me, but I certainly wouldn't volunteer to feel that chest pain again like that or have the worry, thinking I was in serious trouble, deciding how long I could hold off before hitting "Call" on my phone. What I felt terrible about was what I said at the end of the reading. I was talking about the pain earlier in the reading and saying sorry for coming across a bit slow or distant, and then I said this:

> **"I hope that wasn't someone telling me they died of a heart attack because they can piss off! That Hurt!"**

To say I felt guilty for saying that is a huge understatement and typical of me sometimes putting my foot in it. I was a little bit of a nervous wreck now, just not knowing what was coming next and where from. Then this happened...

I must be very vague with this one as there is still a murder investigation ongoing, so I need to be careful with details. While a client I was talking to was talking about a family member who was on a trip, I became aware that this relative had been separated from the person he was with and was now in Spirit. The person being talked about by the client was now dead and the client was unaware.

How do I tell someone that if I am wrong? I need to be very sure I have this right now if I am to pass this and, even if I do, is it even my place?

I did not know what to do, but the names Spirit gave me, and in turn passed to the client, opened a can of worms that became very complicated. It really made me question what gave me the right to do this in the first place.

After that event, and incidentally receiving rather negative feedback from someone else I read for whilst having a bad day, I became mentally drained. At this stage I was completely overwhelmed, hurt by negative feedback, and at the stage where I was questioning why I wanted to do this in the first place. As much as I had tried, I had still failed. Imposter syndrome set in and despite all the people who were grateful for the readings, there was no way I could get out of this frame of mind. The few negative events completely took over my mind.

I took a period of time away from it because of mental exhaustion. When I got to the date I had planned to return, I had to extend that time as I was just not in the right place still. I was still picking up loads of messages for people around me and had no problem with off-the-cuff readings at all! This was clearly because there was no pressure.

The thought that got to me most was taking money for a reading and worrying that this could be someone sitting there ready to test me or prove me wrong. It just hammered away at my confidence to the point where I had to refund months of bookings and close up shop for the time being because I was in no state to do this while my head was in this place.

I will explain the issue I had in more detail and how it connected to mental health in a way that I really hadn't ever thought about in the past until I started looking into it more. My mental state had made me physically ill to the point where I was completely run down and had a weakened immune system.

I had tormented myself and tortured myself so much that my own negative thinking had made me sick...

6.

THE EMOTION BEHIND ILLNESS

I have an app on my phone where people in my town can contact each other on a forum to ask things like where to find a roofer or who hasn't cleared up after their dog. Maybe even so Betty at number 45 can voice her frustration with the owners of number 43 who play their music too loud, that sort of thing. I'll be honest; I find it very entertaining to scroll through at times. Like others I'm sure, I find it entertaining when such small things to some get such an angry reaction from others. Coupled with the comments and responses from other neighbours, it can at times be a type of people watching.

I was scrolling through recently and read a post from a man who was clearly new to the app, possibly the area too. He was just saying hello and that he was happy to help locally if anyone was in need. It was very nice of him and he seemed like a good man.

However, he did feel the need to mention the fact that he was doing God's work so that he didn't burn in hell...

"Hang on a minute there, buddy... WHAT?"

I had to open the comments section for this one... How was there a message about burning for eternity nestled between one post about someone stealing doormats and another post asking if anyone knew a good cleaner? I suppose it's why I like this app. He was asked what he meant by that, and he explained his "facts" like this: "We are all destined to burn in hell. But by doing God's great work we can be spared from this eternal punishment; this is what makes us good people."

So, you needed a threat of burning for eternity to be willing to help an elderly neighbour? Is this not a completely insane way of looking at things or is that just me? I think I'd help the neighbour regardless of what comes in my afterlife, but that might just be me, what do I know?

This was his reality. He offered no proof to substantiate this "fact" that he had told the group, let alone how he knew this, or offer any other form of explanation. It was like he was helping people out by letting them know that if they do God's work, they will be spared this eternity of burning in hell. I mean, yes, OK, you might not have proof to hand, but surely a rational explanation of why you are so sure of this other than "This is the fact". A fact that has been told to you repeatedly since childhood I would imagine.

"Who told you that, mate? And how do they know for sure? Because to say something that is so fear-inducing, surely you have some strong evidence to go with that statement? Are you aware that a human can be a good person without the need to be threatened with burning for eternity?"

I think the saddest fact about this is that this person was so sure of his "facts". I can only imagine that whoever taught him this was as sure of their "facts".

This, to me, is yet another example of using fear to control whilst thinking we are doing a good thing by our children. The sad fact is we are passing on things we have no concrete proof of. To make this worse, we are instilling a fear of burning in hell just because that's what we were told would happen; I mean is there any documented proof of this occurring? I just can't understand why we would say this without evidence. Surely that puts a huge amount of anxiety on anyone, let alone a child. I cannot imagine looking my children in the eyes and explaining to them that they are destined to burn for eternity and only by spreading the word of God can they be saved.

I know many religious people who do not have this narrative at all, so please do not take this as me attacking religion in any way. My issue is with the way us humans use fear as a means of control. I'm no expert but I'm not even sure hell was in the Old Testament, was it? Is there even the smallest possibility that the story could have somehow been changed over the years?

To a certain extent, I even used fear with my children to control them. Not in the same harsh way but a less drastic version. If you have children, have you ever said the words, "Behave or Santa won't come"? I know I have and it was a very useful tool for the last three months of each year while they were younger to get them to behave better. I used fear to control my kids in the same way humans use fear to control other humans and have done for hundreds, if not thousands, of years.

I'm sure the correct way of handling that situation would be very complex; teaching the child "why" they should behave or that Santa coming with presents is something that is merely a reward for good children and something encouraging rather than threatening.

I'm not a child psychologist so will retreat from that subject, but my point was that encouragement hopefully gets the same results without the anxiety served up with a threat. Instilling fear is a way of gaining control and the anxiety from fear leads to disease.

Behave or Santa won't come… Anxiety

Worship and repent or burn in hell… Anxiety

~~Burn Sage or unleash~~… I'm not going there again!

Some things we are threatened with to make us good people, in my opinion, can start the thought process of accepting anxiety as just a part of life. When we have anxiety about the way something could turn out, normally focusing on the worst-case scenario, we become apprehensive or anxious.

We have years of stress and worry; then we hit a period of time in our lives when Spirits see and feel we could do with knowing they are there for us, so they step it up a notch when we are at breaking point. Possibly we suffer a loss also and the person who passed is really trying to get a message to you. Notch it up further in some cases with the stress of a controlling or abusive relationship, then bang! Spirits are more than likely going to step in now, let's hope that doesn't confuse things more…

We start having that awakening and the same thing occurs; we get told things by some people that would have us believe that we are not knowledgeable enough to be worthy of connecting with Spirit until we inflate this particular person's Ego while they tell us the dangers of the Spirit world. We can be forgiven for being too trusting sometimes in what we blindly believe. When I was contacting psychic mediums for the first time and was told how important it was to say protection prayers and sage my house, I became anxious.

I became anxious because for a very short period of time, even though this all sounded like such bullshit, so many people had told me to worry that I wondered if I was wrong. Suddenly, rather than just think that I should say this prayer or burn sage, just in case, I was in bed at night wondering why there would be a negative Spirit coming for me in the first place and if they were coming for me now, what the fuck was going to happen to me when I died?

So, should we just burn the sage, accept that it's helped and move on? Well, yes, if you don't overthink the implications. But we are over-thinkers, so we do. We overthink everything until we do one of two things:

1. We make sense out of it and leave it there, moving on to find the next thing to worry about obsessively because we are born worriers.

2. We freeze mentally, stuck thinking about that one thing because it just does not make sense and fills us with anxiety.

After thinking about things logically, listening to some of these people with their warnings of Spirit, I honestly felt like they had watched too many crap horror films. We are not opening any doorways to evil; we are not opening the gates of hell; **we are not inviting anything to be around us that isn't already there!** We are simply tuning in to something that has been around us since we were born.

There are countless Spirit workers that are fantastic and do such good things for people for the right reasons. Unfortunately, we have to be aware of the ones that spread complete misinformation that adds to that feeling of losing your mind. Even if said with the best intentions, knowledge without proof is just rumour. Millions of lives around the world have been lost due to believing certain things with no proof. Religious wars for one! Then the suicides, starvations, illness through worry, and murders that are a direct result of misinformation.

To be clear, I use the term misinformation for something that is told as a 'fact' with no proof. Some theories without proof may turn out to be true, but is it worth the loss of life before we know for sure?

The fear thrown at us is so dangerous, even though sometimes it's with the best intentions of trying to make someone a better person, as explained perfectly above by the friendly local hell dodger. He meant well and his 'facts' were only 'facts' because of what he was taught. Maybe we all need to be careful when passing on information that we simply can't demonstrate as fact. Offer theories; offer your beliefs, but ONLY offer fact if you can demonstrate it as fact. If we all did that, we would see a HUGE reduction in mental health issues and disease.

As well as control through fear, humans love doing something else too…

Humans love to give pills out to patch over pains and ailments. During my life, I have been obsessed with health, natural remedies, herbal treatments, causes of illnesses and why we need so many pills. In fact, I must be very careful that I don't turn this into a health book now, so I'll be brief.

Something I found to be interesting is the amount of disease I have read about that has been cured with natural methods. Not rumours and tales, but actual funded studies by reputable universities. One thing I am fascinated by is the healing power of raw vegetable juice and one author I was inspired by was Jason Vale. This man was once an overweight ill human with chronic psoriasis who managed to change his life by juicing raw vegetables. He trusted in this and wrote a fantastic book on the subject, even made a film that is shocking; showing how people with different ailments, just juicing for a month, could clear so much and didn't need pills anymore!

Although many medicines are world-changing, life-saving, fantastic advancements that have saved so many lives, I do think the business side of pharma has a big part to play in what we are told in the world of illness. I bought a book that Jason Vale had written called *Slim for Life*. In the first edition, there was a fantastic piece about 40 individuals with a particular disease willing to carry out a trial. All but a few were fully cured, drinking nothing but carrot juice! Unfortunately, I lent the book to a family member and never got it back, so about four years later, while I was talking about how good the book was to someone else, I had to buy another copy just because I wanted to read this thing again to give me a bit of motivation.

The part of that book that stood out to me the most was the 40 patients were nearly all cured fully of a particular disease that makes pharmaceutical companies billions. Well, this was the second edition of that book, that part was now removed! I have not spoken to the publisher about why it wasn't in the second edition, but I just can't see the author removing such a powerful study from his own book. I don't know for sure but have my thoughts about it.

I think the rest of my opinions to do with that story would fill a whole book so I will leave it there, but I strongly feel that much of our 'knowledge' in life is based on the profits of others. Are their facts about some things not facts at all and just what we are taught because that 'truth' benefits someone? Just a thought, but I would love to know who wanted that study taken from the first book and why.

I do think it's a shame that so many drugs are handed out to just hide problems. Take ibuprofen (in the right circumstance) as a very "tip of the iceberg" example. A fantastic drug that reduces pain so we can continue with our busy lives.

Let's say I have a drink problem that leaves me with a pounding headache every morning, leaving me unable to function. These marvellous pills get rid of the headache so I can go about my day! These pills take away all effects from the root cause of my issue and leave me feeling great! What they don't do is take away my alcoholism.

Over time, while the pills work their magic, my liver is degrading and before I know it, I need more pills, or a procedure, or a casket! Even if I need a casket, I will need more drugs to make me comfortable first! The thing that always bothered me about drugs is that so many (or most) of the things we are treated for (and no, I am not saying a broken arm or an actual injury) are things we can prevent or cure, even once they are apparent! It is nice to see alternative therapies slowly finding their way into the standard now, though, so things do seem to be changing ever so slowly for the better.

Why am I talking about health in an awakening book? Because it's my book for a start, but here's the other reason…

When I feel a bit shit, I have to cancel all my readings and let people down because my body and mind is the only tool available to Spirit during a reading. It does not go down well if a client has been waiting for a session for eight weeks, or longer in some cases, only to be told I have to rearrange. Recently, because I was not taking care of myself, as explained in the previous chapter, I was out of this totally for four months. The first symptom of me not being well? Anxiety! From anxiety came self-doubt and then weight loss, headaches, high blood pressure and eventually, because this bout of anxiety had wrecked my immune system due to my white blood cells being busy dealing with all the inflammatory cytokines, I had flu, colds, and a stuffy nose (try meditating with a blocked nose). Every time I started to feel better, something else would put me out again. All of this because of anxiety and a fear of being judged. Proof that you really can worry yourself sick!

This snowballed from what should have been a week or two off to four months of being unable to sit down to conduct a reading. If this was any other job in the past, I would simply have sucked it up and got the job done. I have always worked for myself and being ill is not a reason not to get to work. If my arms and legs work, then I work. I worked from the age of

13, all types of work and all the hours I could fit in. Heavy equipment installations, building sites, bar work, rooftop equipment installations … the list goes on.

Nothing has drained me quiet as much as sitting giving readings. I don't know why exactly but it is hard on you, trust me! There is no way you can give readings of a good quality if you feel like shit in any way at all. This was dragging on now and I needed to sort it out. Working through anxiety has been my cure in the past, I could just carry on. But now anxiety was preventing me from doing my job! The anxiety clearly needed to be addressed, AGAIN!

As I went on, I learned more about why this anxiety, worsened through day-to-day stress, was crippling me so much. I started to investigate what would make me so much more anxious than someone else. It turns out that things from childhood, things I couldn't remember, had caused deeper issues in my subconscious that manifested throughout my life as anxiety. The root cause was never dealt with and the issue could never be fully cured. Sure, in the past I could mask the problem by working through it and getting on with life, but now everything had come to a halt!

The issue of mediumship with anxiety is that there is no mediumship with anxiety; you simply can't work through it! (I'm not talking about the anxiety I pick up on with a client; that is very brief and not harmful to me). I have done a lot of work on myself in the past because anxiety has been an issue my whole life up until a few years ago when I was under the impression I had a grip on things. It crept back up on me and took hold again but thankfully was faster to get through now using the methods I had learned. That was after I decided to stop feeling sorry for myself and do something about it of course. Incidentally, if you struggle with anxiety, I can only recommend that you read ***Stop Thinking, Start Living*** by Richard Carlson. It is a great read that helped me a lot, both 10 years ago and again recently when I had my slip-up, and a book I recommend an awful lot.

While you are in that heightened state of anxiety, or fear or whatever you want to call it, your body releases chemicals into your system that lower your immune system. We live in a world that is fuelled by stress and most of us don't even realise we have anxiety, due to it just becoming our constant state. I have witnessed in my life good, caring people who are always worrying about everyone else and themselves to the point of incapacity. To some extent this can include individuals who bury pain dying younger than the people who I have rightly or wrongly considered "harder or less caring." Not bad people, just people who don't let things get to them as much. People who either work on their anxieties, e.g., through meditation, or people who just don't let the world around them get to them. 'Thicker skinned.'

There is a theory that thinkers, e.g. higher IQ individuals, are much more likely to suffer from anxiety due to overthinking. I suppose that's a polite way of suggesting that stupid people have happier lives because they don't think as deeply, but I don't think it's that simple by any stretch and a very basic way of looking at it. I can't see it having anything to do with intelligence at all, but I can see the link with empathy. In fact, I would go as far as to say that empaths are more likely to be ill and die earlier if they don't take control. Anxiety, we know, causes illness, ESPECIALLY when it comes to empaths. So why are empaths empaths? And what do I mean by empath?

By talking about empaths, I am talking about people who are highly sensitive and a sponge for other people's feelings and emotions. After a lot of reading about the subject of empaths and split views on whether empaths are born or made, I feel I view it like this:

Maybe empaths are born, but maybe if we don't NEED empathy in early life it gets packed away and forgotten about by our happy human bodies that have no reason to be on high alert. But why would we NEED it? What would make someone so sensitive that they can pick up on emotions, read situations and just know what someone's moods or intentions are? Aware of it or not, we can subconsciously shut trauma away. A highly tuned empath is usually that way because they had to learn to be on high alert as a child.

This could be for any reason that would involve a state of reading or assessing situations whilst on high alert, just in case you sense you will need to react or avoid a situation. This could be to judge a situation at school and how to avoid being bullied. It could be that a parent for whatever reason could be unpredictable and switch into a totally different mood and overreact in some situations depending how badly their day went. It could be the case that they became highly alert to situations because they may have had unsavoury characters around with less than the best intentions for them. Usually, this trauma is over a long period of time involving someone you have around you often involved in your life.

Disappointment from a parent not noticing something fantastic you did and not giving you any praise for it but then noticing somewhere you are going wrong and telling you exactly where, is not something I would include, especially if telling you what you have done wrong involves irrational behaviour or shouting and screaming.

That would be, in my opinion, something that would affect your decisions and behaviour later in life. This can, again, in my opinion, create a people-pleaser mentality and a feeling of unworthiness. That in turn can cause you to put partners in relationships on a pedestal, not feeling equal to them or feeling unworthy, even removing boundaries just to keep them happy. If you grew up constantly feeling like you were not good enough, why on earth would anything ever change later in life without intervention and dealing with it? If you are so used to feeling like you are not good enough, it doesn't matter what you do and how good you look because that mindset is deep within you. That is where we need healing and inner work. Why do some people spend so long in the gym, have perfect bodies and great health but still look in the mirror and hate the way they look?

That sounds like an ideal partner for someone with narcissistic traits if you ask me. So, what have you done? Why are you in this position? You have created the same relationship hierarchy that you have always known, through no fault of your own. After all, you haven't had praise or encouragement but always were clearly told where you were going wrong or what you 'used' to be good at.

Let's just look at it this way… If everything is perfect in childhood or early life, why would we need to develop empathy into such a finely tuned tool? And why are empaths more likely to be people pleasers? Some will argue we don't develop it; maybe we don't, maybe we are born with it and I'm wrong about the developing it theory. From experience, I have yet to talk to an empath in detail and there not be some form of trauma that created a need to be on constant high alert, mostly in childhood, sometimes in later life. But there is a pattern, I strongly feel that.

When I was between the ages of around 18 and 20 when my friends and I were going to clubs and bars a lot more, a friend called Lee said something to me I should have thought about more at the time.

> **"How do you always know there is going to be trouble before anything is said? We didn't have a clue it was about to kick off and we wondered what you were talking about when you said to move away."**

I think the time he said this was just after I had got us all to move away from the bar area in a club in Stevenage because I just knew that something big was about to erupt. I had no idea what or with whom, I just felt the atmosphere around me change, or 'get darker'. It's like the sounds around me blur into the background and my heart speeds up, then my ears start ringing along with a feeling of a dark cloud coming overhead, and this all happens out of nowhere. I had never known why it happened or even if it was normal until people started saying things like was said by Lee that day. It was something I never knew was empathy, but I was finely tuned, I think, from the age of around 13–14.

That was because I was bullied at school, attacked out of school, mugged, and knocked unconscious as a 13-year-old boy in town one day by a grown man who wanted some change. Another time I was cornered in a park by an older kid and his mates. He held me down while his mate dropped a brick on my head and then they gave me a good kicking. There was no reason; I think this group of lads saw me on my own taking a shortcut through a park and were bored so decided to beat the shit out of me. I was 13 years old and remember lying in the corner of the park in agony, not knowing if they were gone or just waiting somewhere for me to move so they could do it again; that and my head was hurting because I'd had a brick bounced off it, along with the rest of my body that had been kicked over and over again from head to toe. So I just curled up in a ball and lay there next to a pile of rubble hoping that nobody spotted me and saw what a 'victim' I was!

I used to try to hide all this from my mum because she had enough stress to deal with and, as much as I hate to admit it, it wasn't just Mum I hid that from, it was everyone because my experience showed that admitting to being a victim made it worse. That or I would get quizzed: "Well, people don't do that for no reason. What did you do?" If you have ever said those words to anyone, trust me, people do things like that for no reason.

Moving to live with my dad and Clive for two years and working in that pub certainly helped me learn how to handle situations. It's funny how it is nothing but confidence and state of mind that can help in such a huge way when in a situation that could end badly. Aside from dealing with people in the real world much more, something as simple as learning the meaning of "keep your head up" is such an important thing. It's surprising how something as simple as that can change the way you are looked at by other people.

And yes, I am talking about posture. I've taken enough hidings not to be fearful of confrontations from people; I just needed to stop asking for them by staring at the floor all the time like a victim. The standing up for myself part, the most important part of it, was soon learned while living in the pub so I was lucky, but it still gets to me emotionally at times how it is for some people.

Maybe all of that is why I find the whole 'dangerous Spirit' thing so laughable. I've never had a gang of ghosts mug me on the way home or anything like that, so if casting a shadow and being scared of sage is as badass as Spirits get, then I think we are pretty safe.

Why would you need to be tuned in to others' emotions so well if you had never been in danger due to someone else's behaviour patterns during your life? My situation isn't extreme at all, people go through far worse than I did, all over the world, so they must have very highly tuned radars. As sad as it is to think about that, it is, unfortunately, how life can fuck you over. This is how we develop our sensitivity to channel and read people so well. It makes us just as sensitive as a new-born baby again, on high alert and having to take everything in to figure it all out. It's not all beatings and abuse either, this can be a subtle change in behaviour over a long period of time due to something we do to others around us that we are not even aware of!

This also includes my children! The fearless connection to Spirit with my kids is natural, yes. But the ability to be so aware of Spirit and read people so well, unfortunately, is more than likely due to the fact that I was so moody during my awakening. No, I wasn't abusive; I didn't do anything other than be in a great mood one day and a really bad mood the next depending on how work went…

Imagine sitting in your room, looking forward to Dad getting home because this morning you were having such a laugh and you want to see him again soon. Now, instead, there is a question mark because you don't know what version of "Dad" is coming home tonight.

Imagine coming downstairs, not knowing if you can be happy and enjoy time with Dad now that he is home because you know it all depends on how his day went. Whether your evening will be fun and happy or stressful and full of anxiety is totally reliant on external things that you have no control over. Imagine getting halfway down the stairs, hearing him moaning about his day, and the disappointment you then feel knowing he's not in the mood today to be the dad you love. More than likely, he'll be shouting at you for something; the same something that isn't a big deal when he's had a good day.

It's not easy admitting, but looking back, I caused my children and wife to become hypersensitive and on high alert at around the time I came home. The kids wouldn't feel the need to come downstairs any longer as time went on because as they were becoming more empathic, they could tell my mood by the sound of the key in the door or how loudly the door closed. Further on in time and developing this hypersensitivity, they would have known how the whole evening was going to pan out just by the way I pulled onto the drive, not even in the house yet.

Once it is established that Dad is in a bad mood today, the high alert kicks into overdrive: Knowing that the jokes you could have told normally you can't today; hoping that the crisp packet just thrown away is in the right bin; hoping Dad don't notice the school bag and jacket just thrown in the corner. Small things that, had my day been going OK, I would have taken in my stride and asked them nicely to correct I would be getting angry about and raising my voice, shouting that I was sick of telling them the same things over and over. This must have been awful for the kids because this is their home environment and although they needed telling, they were usually told in a decent way and still felt loved and secure.

If I came home in a bad mood, I was treating the most important people in my life differently because of a customer at work who did not care about me in the slightest! Before long, the high alert or empathy is so tuned in that we can walk into a room and tell if there has been an argument in there, even if the room is now empty.

Shouting up the stairs to tell the kids off, or not shouting up the stairs, just depending on your mood and how your day went can affect how secure the children feel in their own home. Discipline yes, it's needed for the good of the child, but not erratic discipline that is inconsistent. What does that teach them?

All that disappointment and the anxiety it creates just hoping the atmosphere won't turn sour is something that I am aware of and I realise now how important it is to keep work stress at work. Feeling the atmosphere change is awful for that child and they will do anything they can to avoid that feeling. This creates people pleasing and inequality in relationships later in life, unfortunately, and there's no straying away from the fact that, quite often, if we are highly sensitive or empathic, we are likely to end up experiencing relationships in which we are taken for granted or feel unloved. More than likely, we will have heard the term "needy" too.

I'm grateful I can see what this can do and will do everything with this knowledge to make sure my children do not get affected by the fact that I was a moody arsehole at times. Saying that... They are teenagers now and it's their turn to be the moody arseholes at times, and a nightmare to deal with, but that's karma I suppose. My kids will read this before it goes to print and I'm sure they will agree!

We do everything we can to give our kids a good start, but the little things we don't think of as anything more than a normal response to a bad day can unfortunately, and without being dramatic, change their future happiness.

I did a lot of reading about how other people's behaviours affect our behaviours later in life and how we are moulded. Looking at the types of relationships we enter later in life as a direct result of the amount of love we were shown is crazy! I will always make sure my kids know how much I love them and feel it can be damaging to just presume they know that already, without telling them.

It completely changed the way I looked at myself and the way people around me are affected by the way I have been treated in the past, like a snowball of emotional crap and anxiety getting passed down. Again, I would love to expand on behaviours in relationships and how much our subconscious governs our decision-making when choosing a partner, but it would be best left for a future book.

One thing I was told a lot during my awakening was, "You need to be grounded... Do a grounding meditation... Visualise roots growing into the ground from your feet because you really do need to be grounded." I heard that A LOT, but what does it actually mean? And why do I need to be grounded?

Yes, the meditation helps me work on my Spiritual being and my mind. How about I also do a hydration meditation while I'm at it? You know, visualise drinking a bottle of water, visualise it travelling to my stomach, so I'm hydrated as well as grounded? That way I won't need to drink water, will I?

Oh, that's stupid.

So back to what I was saying about picturing roots. "You need to be grounded." Sometimes I had this explained as simply as, "Meditate and visualise those roots," or, "Put a rock by your bed!" At the time when I was told to put a big rock from outside by my bed, I had to try hard to keep a straight face. I mean as far as I was concerned, my life was falling to bits,

I was losing my mind, and here was a lady telling me to go outside and bring a fucking rock in to put by my bed. *Yeah, like that won't make me look crazy to anyone around me, will it?* But I was being a dick and I don't know; it might be something I'm yet to learn about and I don't see it as a dangerous suggestion. That's until I get up in the night to use the toilet and trip over the fucking thing!

The rock could somehow help in its own way; after all, there are actually certain crystals that make my arms heat up and get pins and needles. I can honestly feel the energy with certain crystals so maybe she was on to something. Crystals, or the term I prefer, stones made from different minerals, actually fascinate me because I do feel energy off these things but won't expand in much detail about that in this book. But the rock by the bed, that was back then, and it is still healthy to look at everything from both sides. So let's look at it from my "PRE SPIRIT-STUFF" point of view, the engineering point of view. After all, we are humans and still have a physical body so let's not get too carried away with the visualisations and feeling energy stuff just yet because as well as the Spirit side we need to look after the Physical with it. The hydration meditation won't cure thirst, will it?

Everyone who tells you that you need to be grounded is correct, I fully believe that. The meditations are good for us, the Spiritual side of us. So, what about the physical side of us? Go for a walk out in nature? Well, yes…

But not in shoes.

You will more than likely know from life in general or a science lesson in school that we are electrical 'appliances. If you don't know that and need proof, go get a multi-meter, put one lead on your skin and the other lead on an earth point. THE EARTH POINT—NOT THE LIVE! If in doubt, just trust what I'm saying: We are electrical 'appliances.

Now, when you look at electrical appliances, unless you have a class-two appliance (we won't complicate this), you will see an earth pin. What does that earth pin do? That earth pin takes residual current or any static current and sends it to the ground. This prevents malfunction and, more importantly, the chance of the user getting an electric shock in case of a malfunction. So, if an electrical appliance needs earthing to prevent malfunction, do we also? We are electrical after all.

Have you ever touched a door handle or anything metal and felt a little shock? That's a build-up of residual electricity that had nowhere to go. When you touch something that is grounded, it leaves you and finds the ground. That residual current is the reason we need a ground lead on most appliances. Even the small amount you can sometimes feel as a static shock would be enough to damage a computer motherboard or printed circuit board in an appliance and our brains have far more circuitry than a computer motherboard, not to mention the rest of our circuitry!

You know when you rub a balloon on yourself, and it sticks to you? Try doing that barefooted on a beach. The static electricity build-up will find earth and the balloon won't stick. So, if we are electrical ourselves, is it not sensible to at least consider how we might need physical grounding to prevent malfunction?

We have two facts here...

We know for a fact that we are electrical, and we know for a fact that residual current with nowhere to go can damage a circuit board. Our circuit boards are pretty advanced, so would it not make sense to think we might need grounding, physically?

Neutrophils are a type of white blood cell and are a hallmark of inflammation, normally around 50–70% of white blood cells. These neutrophils travel to an injury site to repair tissue after an injury. They rip electrons away from the damaged cell and this destroys the cell. We are then left with free radicals that need "cleaning up" with electrons. If there are not enough electrons flowing freely in the blood, they are taken from healthy cells, destroying that cell too. Think about the balloon sticking to your clothes the way an electron would stick to the walls of your blood vessels. If we are grounded, we have more free-flowing electrons for the neutrophils to use, meaning they don't need to destroy healthy cells to get the electrons because they are already there, in the blood. Electrons need to be flowing freely, not stuck to your arteries like a balloon stuck to your jumper with static.

To simplify, if we don't have enough free-flowing electrons, our cells destroy a healthy cell to clean up the mess they made destroying a damaged cell. Now they need to clean up the mess made from the cell they destroyed to clean up the last mess. If there are not enough free-flowing electrons, they have to destroy yet another cell. See the chain reaction? This leads to more inflammation and a whole lot longer to repair than if the body had lots of free electrons moving around in the bloodstream; something that can be achieved with earthing. We fix ourselves faster with grounding.

For us to function correctly for longer, like any other electrical appliance, we need grounding—as much as we can get by all accounts. This grounding gets rid of residual electricity and makes our blood flow better, helping it to carry all the important things, one of which being electrons! This means reduced inflammation, and reduced inflammation means less pain and less disease. Also, if you have a lot of stress, a lot of physical grounding will help massively!

As much as a grounding meditation is great for our mental health and focus, we need physical grounding too because we still have the human to take care of after all. It's the same as my earlier point about performing a hydration meditation and not having to drink water ever again because it's not practical.

You know the times you go on holiday and feel so good while you are there on the sand or in the sea and everyone says how the sun is so good for you because you feel great after? I personally don't think it's all to do with the sun. Think about how often you have actual direct contact with the earth without shoes? All that time on the beach is a lot of direct contact with the ground that you may not be used to, so another reason possibly that you feel better.

This is all proven, not theories. It's also used at events such as the Tour de France; if a rider falls off his bike and hurts himself, he may be put on a bed that is earthed and hooked up with more earth leads. Why? To reduce inflammation and heal much faster.

Inflammation is the cause of most of the illnesses you could name. Inflammatory cytokines, released into the body at times of high stress, are a cause of inflammation. The positive and negative charges in our bodies, when not grounded, become erratic and inflammation can become out of control, leading to disease.

I first became aware of this after stumbling across a video on YouTube called "15-minute grounding movie" championed by a man called Clint Ober. He explains all of this fantastically and I would recommend anyone take a look. After I watched that YouTube video, I went straight on Amazon and ordered a mat that goes on my bed and has hundreds of woven metal strips in it. The mat has a lead that plugs into a wall socket (only the earth pin), and I sleep grounded all night. Now, I could go for a nice long walk in the park barefooted, but round here it certainly isn't practical, and I would have my sanity questioned in no time at all. Not to mention, I have busy days and my 'normal' work requires heavy protective footwear.

Now, since I bought this mat, my body pains have reduced massively. I have spent my life so far doing manual work so had the usual knee pains and lower back pains for years. Sleeping on this mat has made a huge difference and my sleep is much better. I'm even noticing that I am a different person if I don't sleep on a grounding sheet. A different person in a bad way; basically, a tired, achy, miserable bastard! Now we have grounding to help with damage from fear, anxiety and any other injuries that might occur if you happen to have a big silly rock by your bed!

My main point with all of this is to highlight how serious anxiety and stress are and where they can lead if we are not careful and keep on top of them.

Anxiety and stress are killers, but if we tackle our Spiritual, Physical and Emotional health, treating them all with equal importance, we can completely transform ourselves for the better. If one of these areas is not looked after, it will overlap into other areas in no time at all. There is another thing that helps with all-round health though...

My friend Chad, who I spoke about earlier, has a way with words that sometimes, can be very helpful while sounding quite offensive. I was talking to him one day about being a bit low and getting stuck in my head.

What he said to me would probably seem to be the most insensitive thing that anyone could say to someone that is depressed, but he snapped me out of it completely; for that exact reason...

> **"Maybe you should stop being a fucking pussy and accept that life can be shit like the rest of us have to. So, either cheer up and enjoy the night or go be miserable somewhere else, but don't stand here with a face like that ruining my night!"**

OK, the advice was wrong, but the message wasn't. I found that hilarious and, that night, it was what I needed to hear.

I burst out laughing thinking about him working as a councillor and passing words of wisdom like that but, to be fair, he snapped me out of a really shit patch, and it was probably the best thing for me to hear at that time. I can hand on heart say that the night out and a good laugh, washed away weeks of depression that had left me feeling like utter shit.

Friends don't always have to say the right thing. Sometimes the completely wrong thing is all you need, but if you can get out and enjoy yourself, it will work wonders for Mental Health.

7.

ADHD AND YOU AND ME!

"ADHD is an excuse for naughty kids to be naughty."

It's an awful way of looking at it, isn't it? But it was my view completely. That was until I was diagnosed with adult ADHD. Well, there's some karma for me! You see I had heard that phrase somewhere in life and their explanation just sounded plausible, so I ran with it without giving it deeper thought. My whole book is about giving things that we are taught deeper thought, and I missed the fact that I do this myself.

Exactly why I said at the start that I will be learning for the rest of my life.

I will be honest though… Had I been diagnosed with ADHD as a child, I would have had a great excuse. I laugh thinking about how much use to me that diagnosis would have been back then. I would have had an excuse to be the nightmare I was. Personally, thinking back to how I was as a kid, I would have milked it for everything I could.

Or possibly I might have got the attention I needed to get more from my education. Maybe with that extra help, I would not have written what I did in the second chapter about not fitting a mould at school. I may well have fitted the mould perfectly and settled into life like everyone else.

That last paragraph, for me, opens two routes of discussion, both of which, I feel, are very important points to talk about.

This is where I will show why I feel it is so important to view both sides of any argument. We have no right to argue a case or offer an opinion if we don't look at both sides. Just my opinion at the time of course, but I always said ADHD was just an excuse for naughty kids purely because I was "taught" that by someone and did not use my own brain to explore the reason why I held what I now see as a closed-minded opinion.

The general view that made me think the above is, yes, that naughty kid that's a pain in the arse now has an excuse to do what I can't do. He's got a passport to carry on being a pain in the arse while I get called a failure, lazy, and am told I will be on benefits for the rest of my life because I cannot pay attention in your class.

It was jealousy!

You see, I was a pain in the arse too, but I had no excuse. I was too self-conscious due to bullying and several other things and that made me mask, and I masked things very well! I masked things well because of this constant state of high alert and the fact that when I wasn't being a clown, I was in self-preservation mode, and that involved me NOT acting out, pushing all that hyperactivity into my head and blending into my surroundings so I didn't stand out. Apparently even acting the clown was, for me, blending into my surroundings.

My psychiatrist, during diagnosis, carried out a cognitive function test and explained something to me that was very interesting. On paper at least, I am a genius. I honestly feel like a dopey, clumsy idiot, but I wanted to understand why I now had a bit of paper saying I was a genius. Surely if I was a genius, I would be a multimillionaire by now living a relaxed, stress-free life?

As he explained to me why this was so important, I was learning things about myself that were starting to click into place massively. Possibly not for the same reasons he was intending, I should add, because I don't like the idea of someone having a label just because their way of thinking doesn't fall in line with the rest of the world. I knew that it was wrong to be a nasty person all the way through my life, I do not believe that a condition can be used as an excuse to cause anyone else physical and emotional pain. Yes, I say things that I find funny that can be very dark and at totally the wrong times, massively putting my foot in it. But to deliberately hurt someone with my words or actions just is not something I could do. We know that any learning or functional or behavioural condition or however we want to label them is something that makes us look or seem a bit different as children and sometimes in adulthood but not as often.

He explained that because my cognitive function test came back on paper at least, as me being a genius, it made things harder. Rather than always acting out or being overly impulsive, it was my mind that was over-active because I was blending in with my surroundings so as not to stand out, offering myself out as a victim. I was overthinking and people pleasing, yes, but also, because my brain just won't ever shut the fuck up, I look like I'm not listening or paying attention when people are talking to me. The truth is I will be listening, yes, but also dealing with all the other shit going round in my head at the same time.

MASKING!

I struggled to work for anyone at all because if I had a differing view, or what I was being told to do seemed to be an "arse about face" way of doing it, I could not help but mention what I thought and quite often that won't go down very well if you are being paid to shut the fuck up and do your damn job. This is why I struggled in lessons with boredom and could not get my work done. This book is the first thing I have ever written in my life that was more than two sheets of A4 paper because I was passionate about it getting done, not because I had to do it to tick a box.

Now, being a people pleaser who is aware that the way I want to act is not how I should act is the part of this that makes it harder. Apart from me not being able to keep my mouth shut and saying exactly what I feel most of the time, I can pretty much keep the rest of my impulsiveness under wraps, leaving all that hyperactivity in my head, which eventually leads to anxiety and depression because you are not expressing yourself and keep getting asked, "What's wrong with you?" because you don't appear to be focusing when most of the time you are.

That's as a kid anyway, I couldn't give a monkeys if I look miles away now because people know what I'm like and I feel more comfortable because I choose my environments. Unlike my school days, where I had no choice of environment.

I saw a connection between my adult ADHD symptoms and the psychic medium thing…

Not just the ADHD thing either, this could be a host of differing neurodevelopmental or neuropsychiatric conditions.

Interrupting sentences because you will forget what you were going to say if you don't or because you know what is coming…

A very high chance of also having bipolar disorder (this didn't surprise me at all) …

Getting bored because you know what the story is before it's been told so you just shut off…

Being miles away with your thoughts…

Changes in mood so drastic that it feels like someone else's, that you have absorbed…

Having a million things going on in your head at once…

Almost as if there is a psychic thing going on … no?

We all have this ability, but there certainly seems to be a pattern with the ones who are more sensitive!

"But Sean, you said that empathy came from trauma."

This is the most interesting part...

Misdiagnosis of ADHD is very common. Why? Because the symptoms of ADHD are very similar to the symptoms of many types of abuse. Anxiety is the main thing here but that also is a by-product of abuse.

There's also drug abuse, narcissistic abuse, alcohol abuse, emotional abuse, and so many other types of anxiety causing issues. Other people's behaviour during your life changes the way you behave and causes you to be more highly tuned in (including your own behaviour in the case of drug or alcohol abuse). Couple that with the fact that Spirit is trying to reassure you that you have support around you and you have yet another pathway carved out into a spiritual awakening.

Now, I'm not suggesting that every light worker has ADHD, OCD, bipolar or depression, but there is most certainly a link to highly sensitive people and neurodevelopmental or neuropsychiatric conditions. It's such a shame that this is a reason for some sceptics to say we are nut jobs, and this is all rubbish. Possibly I was one of those people, but I have passed too much evidence now to be budged at all. I am in no doubt whatsoever that Spirit and Spirit work is most certainly a fact.

And I need to post the text below from nhahealth.com that talks about ADHD and the way our brains naturally slip into the Delta Frequency!

"We increase Delta waves in order to decrease our awareness of the physical world. We also access information in our unconscious mind through Delta. Peak performers decrease Delta waves when high focus and peak performance are required. However, most individuals diagnosed with Attention Deficit Disorder naturally increase rather than decrease Delta activity when trying to focus. The inappropriate Delta response often severely restricts the ability to focus and maintain attention. It is as if the brain is locked into a perpetual drowsy state."

The Delta Frequency (or the line that crosses Theta and Delta) is a trance frequency. One where we are in the perfect zone for contacting Spirit!

One more thing to think about; if so many cases of ADHD are misdiagnosed symptoms of abuse or trauma of one kind or another, could it be possible that a young child with an ADHD diagnosis, with no history of trauma in this life, could have abuse or trauma from a past life that hasn't healed? Therefore also getting a 'misdiagnosis'? I personally couldn't argue the case for that one way or the other, but it is something I think is an interesting thought.

I am actually very excited about a theory to do with the whole subject of neurobehavioral and neurodevelopmental disorders and currently hyper focusing on theories from different experts.

Something that really interested me is the fact that once I was diagnosed, I was getting this shown a lot in readings. You see, the way I understand mediumship is that Spirit only has one toolbox to use when connecting to this 'dimension'. That toolbox is also the medium's toolbox, their information bank if you like. This will be explained more in the chapter explaining how it works for me, but Spirits need you to have images and information in your head that they can flick through and put forward for you to use as evidence.

Quite often talked about in mediumship is symbols and how Spirits use them to pass information. Previously, when talking to a client with ADHD, I would have no symbol for something like ADHD because it just wasn't available in my toolbox (or in my recent memory). Now I do have this symbol I am discovering something interesting to me that I will no doubt hyper focus on in the very near future when I start pestering parapsychologists to find one to help me with a study that I am desperate to see happen. Before my diagnosis, I had no reason to have any knowledge of ADHD or any connected conditions for that matter. It just wasn't in my toolbox so I would not get shown that by Spirit.

On my own journey of understanding behaviours and why we humans are so different in the way we think, probably because I was diagnosed with a particular condition that made me hyper focus on any particular subject that was new to me and grabbed my interest. I would do this with anything until I absorbed as much information as I could and then got bored. I do think there is so much more I would like to write about this subject also.

Moving away from that for the moment...

One area that did grab my interest was the link between Spirit workers, depression, and the need to replace whatever it was that was missing in our bodies. As far as I could tell, in a lot of cases, whatever was missing could, as we already know, cause depression. They say that serotonin and dopamine are the only two things that can cause happiness. Anything else that you think makes you feel happy is nothing more than a tool to increase one of these chemicals in your body.

I strongly believe that we need to remember the fact that we are a human body while we are here. Remember my point earlier in this book about the grounding meditation? I always dealt with depression by accepting it and making sure I was in the gym every day at 6:00 a.m. If I did that, my mind could cope with anything else in my head because I had the confidence and everything else just bounced off me after a good session in the gym.

In the two hours between leaving my house to be walking out of the gym, I could transform from the most self-loathing, depressed version of myself to someone who could handle anything and felt on top of the world, full of confidence and ready for anything that day. That is fine, but what about the days I didn't go? They were shit days and, to a certain extent, they still are. But surely I should be able to be happy on days that I don't get to the gym? Is this masking something else?

I 100% believe that exercise is essential to us to maintain mental and physical health, that's a complete no-brainer. However, what I am trying to say is this:

Missing one day at the gym should not leave me feeling like a complete failure of a human being for the rest of that day. I can't help thinking that there must be more to it than exercise to keep us happy. Maybe it's a combination of several things that possibly we overlook. Could the obvious benefits of getting to the gym and staying fit also be a mask so that I can avoid dealing with other issues? After all, an hour in the gym cures everything!

What is important to remember here is that when we avoid dealing with things that have affected us, or we just don't know there is anything there to deal with, it is not just us that suffer, it's those around us too. I had no idea that the way I acted in life was because of things I never even remembered. I mean why would something that happened at school affect me now? Unbeknownst to me, an event that gave me a certain way of thinking most certainly had an impact on people who love me. I will explain exactly what event very shortly, but one article that I read recently made me think much deeper into it.

As I read more and more about all of this, I read something that, although it makes sense to me now, I would never have considered in a million years.

Milk intolerance…

Where does it come from? I mean, OK, my common sense says to me that a cow has multiple stomachs, and we only have one to digest it. Then there's the fact that we are the only animal that drinks milk past infancy. (Unless they are given milk by a human.)

We don't all have milk intolerance so I doubt that would hold much ground because we certainly do all only have one stomach. When I read the following, it made me think deeper about the link between emotions and how they can affect us physically:

The article suggested that milk intolerance could stem from the trauma experienced at the time of weaning, if Mum wasn't able to produce enough milk during breastfeeding. The trauma of being pulled away from a food source by Mum, the person you rely on to keep you alive, causes the body to associate milk with being deprived or deserted, in turn rejecting it to try to protect from this feeling.

All subconsciously of course and only a theory with small amounts of evidence for now, but very interesting to read and give thought to. It really does make you think about the degree to which small events in life could have a damaging impact without us even knowing. I strongly believe that EMOTIONAL DAMAGE MAKES US PHYSICALLY ILL, far more so than we currently realise.

Now, if that is remotely possible, and that baby is affected later in life by that, how could that possibly be remembered? And why would anyone link that with emotional security issues later in life? These things, as detailed above, had led me to explore the whole subject of events we are unaware of during early life that affect us in later life.

I was hoping with this awakening stuff that a healer would just touch my shoulder and all of a sudden, I would be a new person with no stresses and an abundance of joy and lots of other lovely things, but it wasn't that simple because nothing ever is…

We need to learn about us; why we behave in the ways we do and why we treat people in certain ways. Once we do that and understand WHY we need the healing and mindfulness, the chakra stuff and meditations will come in much more useful. How can we heal if we don't know what we are healing? Surely Spirit wants us to pull our finger out of our arse, just slightly, to do even just a tiny bit of the legwork.

Otherwise, what have we learnt? And what good does it do us?

The following is an example of something I strongly advise you don't do! It is something I should not have done and would NEVER encourage it.

I had been reading a lot about shaman practices one week and had also been watching a documentary about a group of people who had been treated for depression using LSD. I found this fascinating because during some points in my life, I have been extremely low! Me, being me, I became very curious and wanted to dive a bit deeper into how vivid an experience this could actually be. Having to know exactly what the risks and dangers were, I started doing my homework. As I had never really read about it before, I just presumed it was a drug that made you look a bit crazy and made you see things that weren't there.

Hang on…

I HAVE felt crazy and I'm certainly seeing things that are not there…

Maybe there is something in this…

Have I already been high for the last few years?

Let's face it, the only thing separating me from a secure hospital at this point is a client nodding and telling me that what I just said makes sense. Even though I giggled while I typed that line, it could be scarily accurate!

So I was on my own in the house one night, after watching this documentary a week or two earlier, and decided I'd have a try. Actually, I had decided about a week before when I started to make enquiries about how to get this stuff. I felt totally safe after reading a lot about it and what the process actually is. But at the same time, I should have had company in case I decided I could fly and climbed on the roof to show everyone how well, but I'm a grown man and not a drama queen so I thought it would be OK.

The following explanation is in no way an endorsement of taking recreational drugs but one I will tell only because I think it will stop anyone having to do it (or something responsible sounding like that).

I sat on my bed with this little square on my tongue knowing I had a long wait now before anything was supposedly going to happen but trying to be very professional about how I went about it all as I knew this could be a bit nasty if the conditions were not right. I then fell asleep, and, like a complete dick, it would appear I swallowed it, great start!

When I woke up, it had clearly started taking affect. I think the first couple of hours were spent touching my skin on my arms while thinking how sensitive everything was. It felt like someone had adjusted my colour and brightness settings too. My eyes felt like they were running at 100x power and I was seeing details in things that I had never noticed before.

Something that I also noticed, which I would love to understand in more detail, is the fact that while everything looked super clear and in full HD, my fingers were slightly out of focus and seemed to be vibrating at some high frequency that freaked me out a bit. I literally couldn't focus on them! If anyone does have a genuine answer for that, please do get in touch with me because I would love to understand why that was happening when everything else was in amazing HD.

I was apparently tripping now, I mean I could hear the electricity flowing through the house, of course I was tripping! I was keen to get started with everything I had planned for this experience so I lay down and decided I would try to meditate and see what happened. It wasn't overly a meditation, but I had a lot come through like it would in any other reading. However, this was a free for all! No specific client and a complete open door with my light on so bright that I could have been painted red and white and put on a cliff to keep ghost ships safe!

I asked if there was anything that anyone would like to say for anyone I hadn't picked up on in the past. An old school friend's dog appeared first, randomly! I texted my friend at the time and every detail I gave him about the toys and things connected to his dog, that had passed probably 20 years ago, was correct.

So there was my first major confirmation, maybe this is why the shamans loved their psychedelics!

There was a lot of evidence that came through that night for others, I mean an awful lot! All confirmed to me when I relayed it to the people it concerned. It really was like when I give any other reading but in HD, with surround sound! When I settled and was obviously over the ridiculous peak of this experience, I asked another question…

"What do the Spirits around me need me to know or do for my greater good? And what can I do for you?"

I then decided, after stating my intention of working on me, to try again to meditate. For the first time in four years after his passing, my dad came through, vividly! Yes, I'd had the few words in the past, as explained in previous chapters, but nothing more than that.

I was obviously very emotional because it was so vivid. He showed me things that made no sense to me at the time; he also gave me messages about personal problems I was having and things that did make sense. One of the things he showed me that made no sense at all was a situation in my school days. He showed me that I had been beaten up by someone I trusted massively during my childhood, a close family friend who was two years older than me. I was shown the trauma it caused and how I had trapped emotions and feelings of being turned on by anyone I have trusted in life because of an event I can't remember!

It can't have happened; I would remember something like that, surely?

Well, it did happen. I spoke to my mum after this experience, and she couldn't believe the fact that I just could not remember it! My mind had shut it out, but because my subconscious certainly hadn't, I was going through life expecting to be hurt that way again by anyone I trusted. Waiting to be dropped, let down, turned against, or anything like that. My mind had put this away so I didn't have to live that trauma out again, leaving me to focus on moving forward. However, it hadn't cleared it from my subconscious; I hadn't dealt with it!

There was so much more that evening, but I won't go into details with everything. What was interesting to me was how many things were confirmed to be true after the event. This one part of the experience helped me understand that the times I was told I had trapped emotions or trauma I had not dealt with were far deeper rooted than I had ever imagined!

Do not get any ideas thinking you could be the world's best medium with this stuff. It took me far too long to feel normal again and there is no way I could sit and be present with someone while it was all going on, it would have been very apparent from looking at my face that I was completely wasted! It was a massive task just texting a friend, let alone the thought of sitting and acting normal for someone. On top of that, I was wiped out for nearly a week after before I felt fully back to normal. What goes up must come down, and my word did I come down! I had found out a lot about myself while trying out LSD, but my conclusion is that it was a lazy way of achieving the same result I would achieve if I meditated more, and without the huge comedown to make me feel like shit after.

Again, for legal purposes, this part of the book is complete fiction, officer!

My advice... Stick to meditating...

8.

MEDITATION... HOW BORING!

Firstly, if you are like me you will feel like skipping this entire chapter because, like me, you may struggle with meditation. Mainly because it's so hard to stay focussed and get anywhere other than to sleep! I had a period of time when I would have huge anxiety at the thought of meditating because I knew I was pressuring myself for a result!

The benefits call for a whole chapter, so I recommend sticking with it and I promise not to drag it out too much; in fact, 12 heavily spaced pages are easy, you're welcome! People who meditate are scientifically proven to be happier and healthier; that alone should be enough motivation, but I will do my best to explain how I went from dodging meditation at all costs to embracing and loving it.

You probably realise by now that it won't be the usual "focus on your breath and clear your mind" stuff that I read so often. Once I knew WHY I was doing it and the benefits, I was happy to be meditating at every opportunity, so let me explain why...

At the start of my awakening, I was told constantly to meditate, like it was something I should just shut up and do. Never mind the details, just do it because you're having an awakening and that's what you should do. It's good for you and you will get answers! Once I was told this a few times, I understood the importance and then started putting pressure on myself.

We get told to sit and focus on our breathing and clear our minds. All I ever used to try this for was to contact my guides or Spirit in general and because I knew how important it was to clear my mind, I couldn't clear my mind if my life depended on it!

The best way to describe how it was for me would be to tell you right now that, whatever you do, don't think of an elephant wearing a pink skirt...

Don't picture the elephant or the pink skirt, OK? Not picturing that will be good for you. Are you sure you haven't got any thoughts of elephants wearing pink skirts in your head? Because if you have, you just failed at not picturing an elephant wearing a pink skirt!

Trying to meditate and following instructions to the letter is what, for me, made it so much harder. But when I was supposed to be focussed on something important, I could end up drifting into my own world for an hour by accident. How was it so easy to be in my own world when I shouldn't be but as soon as I sit down to TRY it becomes impossible? One thing I tell clients a lot is something that I discovered one day during my day job...

I was driving from site to site worrying that I had readings that evening and running out of time due to being held up. How was I going to find the time to fit a meditation in before I started? "Tonight is going to be a disaster; I have no time to meditate!" As the day went on, I just accepted that I was going to struggle with my readings because I was running out of time to "clear my mind" when I got home. The drive back from my last job was about an hour and a half, meaning I was due to get back around 20 minutes before my first reading and I still needed to eat and sort the schedule out.

By the time I did get home, it was later than that, but I felt chilled and just jumped straight into what was to be a very successful reading. Even though I had missed my usual mind-clearing meditation, everything was perfectly fine. What happened? Was I lied to about all this? No, I wasn't lied to; we certainly need meditation to be able to see what Spirit is showing us. So why was everything OK? More than OK, the evidence was fantastic, and my clients were all happy.

What I realised was that I did meditate, I just wasn't aware of it. That drive home I was talking about; I was in my own world. It was the type of long drive that when you get to where you are going, you can't remember the journey. Meditation is essentially focusing on a mundane task to rid your mind of other thoughts and regulate your brainwaves, slow it down if you like. I drive a lot and the mundane task of driving for an hour and a half on a straight road was all I needed to clear the stress of the day and leave my mind clearer.

If you drive yourself, you will probably be aware of how you feel after a drive on a long, boring road. You may feel the same as you do after a meditation, like you need to have a good stretch and wake up. That's because your mind was more than likely in the same place as it is when you meditate, but rather than the focus being on breathing, it was on driving.

Driving is just one example, but that day I reaffirmed to myself how important meditation is at the same time as realising how much the pressure of meditating actually affects meditating when we are so new to it. I even got to the point where I was avoiding the word "meditate" and just sitting with myself for a while to chill.

I tried so many different meditations for so many different reasons and found a few that were fantastic for me. The important detail is that they were fantastic for me. Visualisations, I believe, are individual and you have to try a fair amount before you find what is effective. Also, what I find important to stress is that meditations are not all about contacting your 'guides' or whatever Spirit 'contact' you may be trying to achieve.

Meditation, for me, is for my mind and to prepare myself for Spirit connections. Let's face it; I would look a bit silly having to be in a full meditation during a Zoom reading to contact Spirit, wouldn't I? I will explain below to the best of my knowledge exactly why I feel meditation is one of the most valuable things you can do for yourself, even if you take all this Spirit stuff out of the equation totally.

Our brains work mainly on five frequencies or EEG (speed or stress rate to simplify) and the below figures are rough guides, e.g., with Gamma and Beta, either can be active at 30Hz.

Gamma: Anywhere above 30 Hz.

This is usually intense focus and "the zone" if you like. Maybe an athlete in a competition, or an air traffic controller that has a very busy period of time.

Although effective when needed (like fight or flight), this is not somewhere you would like to remain for very long periods of time.

Beta: 13–30Hz.

This is the day-to-day, wide-awake frequency that is heavily associated with stress, anxiety, depression, fear, mood swings, anger, and any other emotion you could imagine in a wide-awake, alert state. To be fair, there are massive differences along the Beta range but generally this is you awake and functioning.

This is where most people spend most of their time and it is also linked to a lowered immune system because we tend to be more stressed in this state.

Alpha: 8–13 Hz.

This is what I consider the minimum level needed for meditation. This is the brain frequency usually achieved at times of meditation or a deep relaxation. This state is very good for memory and learning. Interestingly, this is where fears, habits and stress start to disappear, and your mind can stop with the stress and anxieties of life, enough to start to rejuvenate and repair, or rest.

Surprisingly, this is also the frequency of learning and is very useful in the classroom when younger so a massive endorsement for schools to be a calm and relaxing place!

Theta: 4–8 Hz.

Scientists explain this state as a very rewarding state with dream-like imagery. I agree totally and it's a floating feeling with complete calm and relaxation. This is the space required in your mind to connect with Spirit on a stronger level. This is the area you would be looking to get to for trance mediumship and is something I have achieved on occasions, but I have also fallen asleep on far more occasions while trying! If you ask your higher self a question if meditating in this state, you will get an answer!

Delta: 0.5–4 Hz – Deep Sleep, Deep Trance, or ADHD focus.

From what I could understand, this is either dreamless sleep or a deep trance. It's argued also as a natural state for individuals with ADHD to drift towards when trying to focus.

The Alpha-Theta state is where we normally are when meditating. The reason I feel all this is so important to explain is because I was so stubborn with my avoidance of everything to do with meditating until I knew the details myself. Just because I was receiving Spirit contact without meditation, I was avoiding it and missing out on so many more positive benefits.

Having known nothing but stress and pressure for as long as I can remember, meditation was completely alien to me so the first time I meditated for an hour, it was like I didn't know what to do with myself and ended up stressed because I wasn't stressed! I had a huge feeling like I was forgetting to do something. That helps to show how much I, and more than likely most of the population, was currently coping with this silent killer that is stress and anxiety.

Your brain has two sides...

The left-hand side (hemisphere) - This is the logic side, where things like maths equations, languages, reality-based problems and all the clever, sensible stuff takes place.

The right-hand side (hemisphere) - This is the side of your brain where your creativity and intuition happen. Most important is that this is the side that connects to a higher consciousness. Very useful when you are a medium.

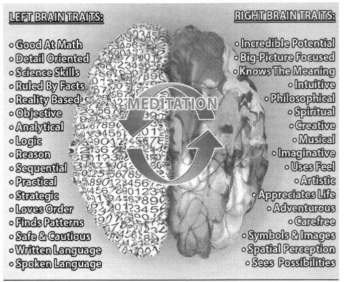

Credit EOC Institute

When we are stressed or just busy with life, our brain functions like two separate machines, not in harmony.

There have been studies showing the brain activity of a stressed-out human being and then the same brain after meditating. You can see in before and after scans how meditation has a brain now working in synchronisation, reducing stress and resulting in a far more efficient brain in general.

I have used a sound collection from the EOC Institute in the past. They have a product called Equisync that I have used to get to the required frequency for easy and effective meditation. I also have some go to meditations on YouTube that are just sounds at certain frequencies that help 'numb' my brain.

Some would call it cheating, but the use of binaural frequencies is a fantastic way of getting your head to the right place, and for me personally it allows me to get to a level of meditation that would otherwise take me years to perfect. OK, yes, cheating I suppose!

A sprinter taking a performance enhancer to get a better time on the track would be banned from the Olympics for doping. Thankfully you can't be thrown out of Spirituality for 'doping' to increase the effectiveness of your meditations. I think binaural frequencies are a fantastic thing, especially if you consider that our brains generate over 50,000 thoughts a day and most of these are FEAR-BASED! Read that fact above again and see if you can tell me that there isn't a bigger problem with mental health than we would be led to believe!

How scary is it to think that we have thousands of fear-based thoughts a day and what these fear based, chemical-releasing thoughts do to our bodies? How many times can you think of where you haven't been good enough today? Or you told yourself something negative about yourself? How many times have you questioned yourself or cast doubt upon you or a situation around you? This world is hard enough to get through and let's be really honest, we normally encounter enough dick heads around us day-to-day, without having to bad mouth ourselves all the time.

Be aware of it and make an effort to cut it out. As an empath or anybody really, you are more than likely harder on you than anyone else so try to stop that!

During our lifetimes we start to categorise our thoughts into good or bad, focusing naturally on the bad more than we do the good. Meditating takes our busy minds away from the day-to-day human crap that we have built up in layers over the years and lets our subconscious mind have a chance to speak. This is where we have a chance to see our full potential in life without the part of your mind that jumps in and makes everything look like shit popping in to put you off doing something potentially amazing!

You have a fear, depression and anxiety centre in your brain called the amygdala. This part of your brain is responsible for setting emotional preconditions. We all know that emotions get in the way of clear thinking, don't we? Researchers at Boston University carried out a study:

The amygdala was viewed on MRI scans of people who had an eight-week course of mindfulness meditation with before and after scans. After eight weeks, the amygdala had actually shrunk significantly! What more proof would you need? We have a proven cure for stress and anxiety in meditation so why on earth would we not give it a go? Once we are doing it for the right reasons, I feel we will get the clearest answers from Spirit too.

As will be explained in the next chapter, I have some visualisation meditations that are short and used to invite Spirit to draw in more (I am actually asking my mind to focus more because Spirit don't really need to draw in more, it's just a figure of speech.) so I can connect for readings, but 90% of my meditation is for me and my mental health.

Once my mind is calm, the rest is easy, and I get to concentrate on my methods used to give readings...

9.

HOW I CONNECT TO SPIRIT

When I first started getting my head around this, I think the overload made everything a much slower process for me. I remember one light worker, right at the start, talking to me about Archangels and how to work with them and almost in the same breath was then talking about star seeds and my higher self. I really was not ready for all that and it made me question my mental health again. It was just too much for a sceptic and I didn't want to be as crazy as her. How ironic that the majority of my spirit contact now is with Angels around a client! The problem is, at that time, I was a sceptic straight off a building site, wondering if my house was haunted. Even approaching someone to ask if my house was haunted sounded silly to me. All of this was so new to me that my first reaction was, ***This lady is fucking nuts! What is she going on about with aliens and angel doctor people? And what does she mean 'higher self'? I might be going nuts, but this lady is tripping!***

The point I'm trying to make is, depending on how far into this discovery we are, information overload can be a negative thing when someone is just starting to come around to the idea that all this is actually real.

In primary schools, there is a way of teaching called phonics, where rather than teach spelling and the alphabet all in one go, it's the sounds of the words that are taught. Breaking the word down for a child and learning the sounds individually, forgetting the correct letter names and spelling for now; just getting used to the basics, e.g., sounds; helping the child to learn a section without becoming overwhelmed by the details that for now, are not important. They all fall into place later, once the basics are fully digested.

I was the child at the start of my awakening, desperate for information but soon overloaded and loosing sense of things. We do phonics with primary school children because throwing a dictionary at them and telling them to get on with it would be counterproductive to that child's learning. A bit like throwing all the crazy shit at a sceptic right at the start of an awakening and hoping they can figure it all out the next time they feel overly pressured to meditate.

I like to treat this whole thing in the same way phonics are taught to primary school children. I break it down into very simple basics without overloading anyone with the finer details. Trust me; that will all fall in to place once you have had proof of your abilities.

There may be small details in what I say that are very much disagreed with by other light workers, but I do things in my own way, with as much respect. Maybe I do not do the 'Holier than Thou' display of spirituality that I am supposed to, or that some would have me believe, but if I did that, I would look like a dick head because it's not me and I wouldn't be fooling anybody.

At the end of the day, regardless of how we imagine Spirit work, I know, for me at least, that the simple stuff works very well. Break it down into simple steps and forget the complicated stuff for now. Yes, I am aware that there may be some deeper reason for me to be more educated, but I am pretty in tune with my Angels, and they don't seem overly concerned with the way I work. After all, this is about Spirit. If I get too bogged down with all the complicated stuff, I might start missing the point of life and forget to enjoy myself and neglect people around me.

By simple stuff I mean the basics at the start. Believe it or not, bringing family through from Spirit for a client is the easy part of all this, especially once we see how we receive messages. The problem is, I have seen this easy part, turned into such a big scary thing that only the masters and experts can do, you would think it's not that easy, then get stuck into all the other stuff, hoping that you can do the next best thing. This leads to missing what does come through because you automatically expect not to be able to do this! It was certainly easier for me to just "say what I see", than it would have been to master the Tarot, for example.

I used to hear the term, "Every Medium is a psychic, but not every psychic is a medium."   I call bullshit on that... Every single one of us has the same tools and we can all do this if we just trust that we can.

The hard part of Spirituality for me was getting my head around everything else; the deeper stuff like which Archangel is called for what reason, or Akashic records, past life regressions, divination tools and so many other things than can overwhelm if thrown at us all at once.

Once we get used to receiving messages from Spirit, we have access to the best teachers available.

My basic readings have helped a lot of people and given reassurance that the client has Spirit around them, something I have no shame in being proud of. Had I carried out a five-year study into spirituality, making sure I fully grasped every single theory (they are all theories until we see evidence), I would not have been able to pass the evidence that I did at that time to the people who needed the one thing I could do.

Carrying on trying to grasp everything, knowing I wasn't passing what I could get because I was told that I wasn't experienced enough, didn't make sense to me, it felt almost selfish or at the very least self-indulgent. After everything I tried to learn and listening carefully, I found I was most comfortable with passing messages from Spirit. Evidence of something after; that's all I wanted to do because that's where I felt I could be the most help. My Spirituality niche if you like. That is not to say I won't always be learning and improving. If I wasn't, then I would be doing something very wrong.

One thing I will say is that after all the other things I have learned, all the extra details about all this, for me personally it's the basic task of passing messages from Spirit that gives the most comfort to someone. That is obviously only my view, but for the following reasons...

1; I have a client who is in so much pain over a loss that they just need one piece of undeniable evidence that will give them reassurance that their loved one is around. They don't need a performance or a future reading, just some proof. One thing from me that, they know, there is no way I could have known.

2; They think they are bat-shit crazy, and think I am too, just needing that bit of proof to stop them self-referring to a secure hospital.

3; They are just having a shit time, feel low, or lonely, and want evidence presented to them, showing that they have Spirit around them, possibly opening up a whole new way of thinking.

Let's face it, there are far more TV shows about passing messages from Spirit than there are fortune telling's and relationship readings. I feel that is because it is far more valuable to a client to contact Spirit because when we see that, we realise the little things that worry us, that feel like big things, are much easier to put into perspective.

This chapter is about how I connect and every little process I go through before I start a session of readings. The first thing I do is a meditation.

After trying countless visualisations during meditations, I found three or four that I now stick with because they seem to help me connect. The first one I use is very simple: I sit quietly for 5–10 minutes with my eyes closed, focusing on my breathing. What I do during this time is say a few words whilst making the words fit my breath totally. For example, on the intake of breath I would say the words, "Focus on," making those two words fit my breath in perfectly. If I am still breathing in and not saying the words still, I do it again.

On the breath out I can say whatever it is I am focusing on, e.g. "my connection with Spirit." Saying this keeps me busy enough to stop my mind wandering and helps me stay with the task of clearing my head. While I do this, I visualise being immersed in white light and walking into a room that I like to think of as the "waiting room" where Spirit may be present. I combine this with a simple shower visualisation, where I picture myself standing outside during a rain shower but with tiny little droplets of white light falling from the sky instead of rain.

As they fall, I slowly become covered in light and visualise this 'light' rain finding its way into my head, totally filling my head up. I then picture my third eye, open and letting the light back out again, while using that eye to see what Spirits may be sitting in the waiting room. I then say, "Thank you." Any sceptic reading this will be thinking I've finally cracked, but that's OK, I would be thinking the same if I hadn't experienced it and, after all, it's just an exercise to clear my head enough to focus on what's coming through for a client.

Along with the above meditation, something I do often without the visualisations is listen for the ticking clock that is close to where I sit. Something I find very valuable when meditating is when I can no longer hear the ticking from that clock. It still fascinates me that by focusing on my breath and meditating the noisy clock next to my head can in fact become completely silent. Once that happens, I know I am ready to start my readings.

After I have that out the way and I have a client sitting in front of me, I like to explain fully how I work. By doing this and explaining how every image and feeling comes through, I feel that it gives the client a better understanding of how Spirit communicates because I always had the thought that if this was real, then a medium could just have Spirit standing next to them and give every detail with no issues at all. I now know that it really isn't as simple as that and, like I said earlier, during mediumship, we are Spirit's toolbox. Becoming aware of how it works showed me that it's a bit more complicated than that so I will try to explain in the clearest possible way:

We have a TV show over here called *Catchphrase*. The previous host, Roy Walker, used to stand there showing an image that was a clue to the catchphrase that the contestant was supposed to work out. His own catchphrase was, "Say what you see." Well, that's a bit like how it works. I will take everything else out of it just for now and talk about the images and how I see them because we all get this, we just don't know it yet. An awakening, as far as I'm concerned is just Spirits way of stepping it up a gear so that you have to start paying attention.

Your brain is just a box of images and feelings for Spirit to use as props to get information across. Imagine you have a building on the other side of the road and someone is trying to communicate with you from the window opposite. All they have is a box with images in it and feelings written on cards. That is what it's like in basic terms, and your head is the box of props. The more information, landmarks, places, languages, names and feelings in that box of props the more Spirit has to pass a message to you.

I'm going to give an example here while I explain how I work... A male in Spirit that was a bit of a 'badass' has to give me enough information so I can describe him to my client with enough detail that the client knows exactly who this is. This 'badass' will start giving me the goosebumps feeling on my right side. Now I know this is a blood relative. I don't know why I get the badass feeling, but I trust the feeling as I just have the feeling he was someone who could handle himself and was not to be messed with; hopefully he will give me a bit more about that as we go on. On that side, I also have two corridors, Maternal and Paternal.

Due to Spirit's positioning, I can now be sure that this person was a maternal blood relative as opposed to a paternal blood relative who would be showing on the left corridor on my right-hand side. Very rarely have I had any Spirit come through that had passed before my client was conceived, so the person I describe, I would hope, makes sense to the client.

As far as relying on pins and needles or goosebumps on a particular part of my body to tell whether I have a blood relative or not is something I trust 100%. If that person in Spirit is presenting on my right-hand side, then that is a blood relative of the person I am reading. HOWEVER, I have had clients on Zoom before that just stared blankly at me and did not have a clue who I was describing. Surprisingly, it sometimes turns out that they have a friend or partner in the room that I can't see on camera and I have been told a few times that the reading sounded like everyone came through for the person I could not see. It's funny how it works and I'll be the first to admit that, with things like that, sometimes it doesn't go to plan.

Again, I will stress that this is how it works for ME, and like I have always said, there is no rulebook. So set your intention with Spirit and see how things build. It took a long time to get the "mapping" figured out, but it is very helpful now.

In fact, I am so reliant on this that I once had a lady sit for a reading and recognise everyone who came through as family members. The only problem with this was that the Spirits came through on my left-hand side, the non-blood relative side. The people she was sure were her blood relatives I was sure were not! It was slightly awkward, but I just explained that I am an idiot on the other side of the world saying what I see and she could take it or presume I was wrong.

It was another thing that made me think to myself, ***Do I have any right to do this?*** I was thinking that because I knew she was adopted, but she clearly didn't. Around a week later, I received a lovely message from the client, explaining to me that, although she always wondered if she was adopted throughout her life, for various reasons she never brought the question up with her parents.

That was until our reading. She told me she could see what I was thinking and decided to talk to her family about it. Apparently, when telling her mother that she had been for a reading and the fact that I had bought her 'blood' relatives through on the non-blood-relative side, she burst into tears. Thankfully they are both fine, but she is adopted. I trusted what I was getting and that was something I took a long time getting used to. It's hard to trust yourself when the client is saying no but I have had too many emails and messages now, days, weeks, sometimes months later saying that what I had said, now makes perfect sense.

I explain that I rely on changes to the feeling of my skin, explaining that if I get goosebumps on my right arm then I have a blood relative coming through. The same on my left-hand side would be a non-blood relative. My back is the clients' Angels, and the front is where I receive information from the client's 'guides'. I say guides but any Spirit giving me current information about the client would be at the front.

As far as I am now concerned, anyone around you in Spirit can take up the role as a guide. Let's say I had a male blood relative come through…

His descriptions of himself would be at my right-hand side, so if I was aware of a white dog to my right-hand side, I would think he was saying he had a white dog. Now, the white dog isn't an image anywhere but in my head. Not literally apparent to my right, I just feel the energy to my right-hand side while I have an image of a white dog put into my head.

If he was to put the image of the white dog into my head and I felt the energy change to the front of me, e.g., pins and needles/goosebumps at my front, I would know this male was telling me something about my client. This would be a way for Spirit to give some evidence to show that they are around by saying that the person I am talking to has a white dog.

So, with this 'badass' on the blood relative side, he will need to see what images I have in my head so that he can put bits together to describe him. So first he might flash just a hair type or something significant at me to get me started. Or I could just get a number that could be an age, let's say 76. The funny thing with Spirits having your head and memory at their disposal to use as a tool for building an image of them up is they certainly find things that were long forgotten to me!

For example, this 'badass' male scanning my head, looking for things to give me to build this picture up, could find an image of Chuck Norris and make that pop into my head. Now, I can be pretty damn sure that this is from Spirit because Chuck Norris doesn't just pop into my head! I haven't seen *Walker Texas Ranger* since I was about 10, so an image of Chuck Norris popping into my head is 100% this man's way of giving me a bit of a description.

I don't normally do the describing rather than saying what I saw if I get someone off the TV because I like to give every detail. So, if your 'badass' grandad wants to give me Chuck Norris as a place to start this connection, that's what I'm telling the client, rather than "Was this man a sheriff and a kick boxer?" because that would be guessing and there may be another reason for being shown Chuck Norris that only the client will understand. Very often the response will be something like, "We always said they looked like that person," or something along those lines.

The only thing that stops this being imagination for me is that these sounds, images, or feelings just pop in fast and then I have to almost do a double take in my head and go back to get it, unlike when I imagine something, it is just there. Add the pins and needles feelings in certain areas of the body and it pieces together very quickly indeed. There are also smells, tastes and sounds. I would go into detailing what all the clair senses are, but I have enough to write here without listing things that you can find in every other spirituality book ever, that would be **'clairboring!'**

I will talk briefly now about being a bit demanding. I hadn't long been giving readings at the time of this next example, but I had put my number as a Google ad locally, offering trust readings, where the customer pays afterwards if they feel it was worth it.

I had a phone call not long after placing the ad from a lady in the UK. I could feel Spirit around at the time, but other than that I was getting nothing at all. I was getting slightly frustrated as I could feel Spirit so why wasn't I getting any evidence? With that thought, I said the following in my head, very loudly…

> **Fucking give me something now, please! You wanted me to do this, but I am starting to look stupid so please give me something or I am never doing another reading again!**

No sooner had I said that, I started getting images through; one in particular was a Second World War prop plane. After that, I was instantly thinking about Duxford Open Air Museum. When I told the client I had an image of a war plane, but a large model replica, and that I felt like this model was at Duxford

Museum, she confirmed that her brother, now in Spirit, had made a model aeroplane. It was a model of the one her father flew in the second world war. She also confirmed that the model plane was, in fact, on display at Duxford Air Museum! To me, evidence like this is complete proof of life after death and something that nobody could argue was a lucky guess.

Had I not put my foot down with the Spirits and asked them to sort it out a bit faster for me, because clearly, they were present, I would not have been able to pass that message to my client and she would not have had such a reassuring piece of evidence; one that she knew, beyond all doubt, I had no way of knowing. She called me out of the blue after seeing a local Google advert, leaving no room for her to wonder if I did my research or anything like that. I had no idea who she was, but her brother and father in Spirit, came through and gave enough to prove to her that they were around still.

This is why I can be a bit stroppy sometimes with Spirit. At the same time, I know that Spirit around me is happy to be guided sometimes, and by that, I mean guiding Spirit with what help we need or "stating our intention". I don't think there is an issue with demanding a bit of help sometimes, if you show how grateful you are after, once the stress has died off.

Something else worth bearing in mind about that reading is the fact that I knew what Duxford Open

Air Museum was. I haven't been there since I was a young boy but the fact I was aware of it meant that Spirit had that in the toolbox to show me. If the model plane was in any other museum that I did not know then the evidence would not have been as detailed. This is, like I said earlier, due to the fact that our heads are Spirit's toolboxes.

The more knowledge, pictures, places, maps, languages, and feelings in our toolbox the more tools Spirit has available to communicate with.

Something I will say again is that Spirit KNOWS us and has done our whole lives. I talk to Spirit like I talk to any of my good friends. We all know we can be a bit stroppy or short at times, but with real friends you can also be yourself and be understanding of one another's personalities. The same way I think it's perfectly healthy to tell someone to piss off and remove them from your life if they are draining your energy. But I normally feel guilty about that after so I can't really sit here pretending to be overly assertive, I just try to be.

Saying what we want, or "stating our intention" to the Spirit around us is very important. As with a lot of subjects in this book, I could write a whole other book just on the subject of this chapter, but if this is new to you, you will not need any overloading for now.

Practice with others and ask them to give you the name of someone they have, in Spirit, that you didn't know. Focus and describe everything you imagine, without cross-examining yourself. Keep practicing and when you do, ask questions:

Imagine what that person looks like and try to build up a picture of anything you can. Write down every-thing: Pets, colours, clothing, random items that flash in, people you imagine around them, how many chil-dren you imagine they had, what they did for work and things like what the decoration in the house may have looked like.

This might sound like a silly exercise but take your time and see how big a picture you can build up of each person. Don't force answers or look too hard, just sit and be aware of what expands while you look at what pops in. Be aware of the fast flashes that you seem to just get a small impression of.

Some days I can look at my schedule for that evening and have names stuck in my head for the rest of that day. Even now as I type this, I am getting a huge pins and needles feeling on the right of my torso, almost as if someone is trying to tell me that they had a pain here and something to do with passing. My head also has pins and needles in a circle all the way round it and when I became aware of that, I knew it is because the first person I am speaking to tonight, either has a headache or has been getting a lot of headaches.

I have a lot to get done before the readings today and I am not offended or concerned with the fact that a loved one is excited about what is coming up later today. There is no need for sage, no need for cord cutting, this energy is not draining me like sometimes happens in readings, but not when I am just 'aware' of spirit around me. In fact, it isn't really Spirit that drain me at all! Normally it is the client's that sit there with their arms folded and unwilling to engage with me, so I can't blame Spirit for that!

Something I will repeat about connecting with Spirit is the following...

Someone dressed from head to toe in purple, putting on a show and paying attention to theatrics, with endless tools and ways to contact Spirit, maybe also warning about the dangers of Spirit contact or why you need to be careful, has no more or a right than you to contact Spirit. All this talk of spirit being dangerous, avoiding divination on Halloween, and the other shit I hear, is nothing more than a way of controlling an 'industry'.

YES, AN INDUSTRY!

Even the history of witchcraft, thanks to humans, and their fantastic way of messing things up, is completely lost in translation! Witchcraft is not a bad thing at all, quite the opposite! In fact, my daughter is a witch as well as a fantastic psychic. Witches get a very bad reputation in history but thankfully as we have come on through time, they are more accepted as the healing, talented beings they are!

No matter how much we believe it and try to make it seem like we have a more extraordinary way of bringing Spirit forward, when it all gets stripped back to one particular fact, it becomes clear that everyone is as entitled and equipped to contact Spirit. A fact that raises doubt with all the other things we are told by some, that would suggest Spirit contact is an exclusivity that only the few can achieve. A fact that means all we have to do, is know what we are looking for to be able to do exactly the same thing.

That fact, is that we all have Spirit around us throughout our whole lives, there for us, and happy to talk to us...

10.

THE SPIRIT AROUND US

I will start this chapter by thanking a client in the USA called Reese. Seeing the stress and confusion that he was struggling with, I became more determined to do this than I could have possibly imagined beforehand, even at the risk of triggering some people around me. Reese had so much information he was taking in, and overload was clearly taking its toll, along with some other personal issues, it was all becoming too much. All I wanted to do, was somehow remind him that life is supposed to be fun, but there was too much going on for that for now, and he was far from having fun. He was in a bad place, and I was genuinely worried about him. Sometimes I just wish I could take a client for a beer and get them away from everything for a while. This was definitely one of them times.

During the conversation, he pulled out a large medical syringe and explained to me in detail, exactly where he could push the needle to end his life, explaining that, because of the way he was feeling, having that choice was comforting for him. If I didn't feel strongly enough about the damage that can be done with misinformation, I certainly did now. He is not the only one that has been here, and he certainly won't be the last, but thankfully he has moved forward and in a better place in life. Awakenings, from what I've seen, can sometimes make everything going on around us worse, while we are trying to work out so much already.

Thank you for opening my eyes wider and reminding me why I'm doing this Reese.

We can be aware of Spirit around us and get so many different explanations for what is going on, that we can collapse emotionally. Because of that, I feel it is so important for us to look at things clearly, taking anyone else's views out of it at first, concentrating on what FACTS we have. Once we clear the crap out of the way and focus on our own connection, things normally seem a whole lot better.

Something I think is especially important with all this awakening stuff is that I think that maybe Spirit would like us to laugh more and take some things less seriously, even if that means having a laugh at all of this occasionally. Spirit knows laughing is good for us; the Spirit around me certainly must have a good sense of humour. Why would Spirit want you to be so serious if laughing releases chemicals that are good for our body? After all, Spirit is there for us.

You will feel much better in yourself if you carry on being you. The best version of you that may have been a bit childish now and again. I know for a fact there is a lot of humour in the Spirit world, I've felt it and witnessed it countless times... One perfect example is the poke in the back story from Ch.4.

While I was looking for answers and looking at all the unusual types of readings we can buy, one thing that did stand out to me was the "draw your guides" or "message from your guides" readings.

I instantly became aware of how many Westerners have wise monks, and Native Americans as guides, and being a naïve, argumentative pain in the arse, I had to ask a few questions about this...

Why are there eagles everywhere? Why are eagles more common in the Spirit world than a pigeon? Why can't my family, that I feel around me, guide me also? Why am I spending all this money trying to get readings to hear what my guides have to say? Is my dad more stupid than the standard non-Western guide image we have come to expect? I have had clients with no interest in their loved ones around them because they were so wrapped up in finding out about their 'guides'.

At the time, I had only ever seen mediums on TV, and not once had any of them brought a guide forward, always just loved ones, so this was all totally alien to me.

This narrative of having a guide that we have never known did not really compute with me at first. Family and loved ones I understood, it makes perfect sense... Watch over those you have left behind and when there is no-one from your time here to watch over, go back and have another incarnation to see if the next life is a better lesson.

And something else about that, something I really cannot get past... In all the readings I have done for people of different races or colours, from all over the world, Race or colour has never been a thing in a reading. I can describe someone in Spirit, but it is almost like race or colour does not exist. From my experiences so far, I can only see it as fair to ask why it is that race is so often mentioned when I hear people describing a guide. Could your Spirit guide, the Native American chief, just be your uncle Bob with a bit of Ego tinkering somewhere? And would that mean old Les from the pub might now be guiding a monk in Tibet? Has anyone ever had their guide drawn for them and they turn out to be just a bus driver from Kent? Or a school dinner lady? Or a streetsweeper? What makes the Tibetan monk or the Native American chief, or even doctor, more important or wise to us? Could this in any way just have an element of Ego interference? And why is race even a thing with guides, when it has never been a thing in my readings?

Please see this for what I am trying to say...

If my experience, validated experience, conflicts with a narrative, is it not a reasonable thought to put out there for debate? In fact, I can only think of one time when it has even come up in a reading and that was for nothing more than to pass evidence.

I had an elderly lady come through for a girl I was reading for, and Spirit told me to say, "White Nana," to pass evidence of which grandma was coming through. I can see why Spirit would give that detail to describe themselves if here on earth they were the only white member of a black family. Probably the best piece of evidence she could pass me in that situation; even though in my head I was thinking, ***Do I say that? Are you sure that's what you mean?*** Out of all the readings, that once is the only time that race has ever been a thing. And that was to identify themselves to a family member here by describing what she looked like when she was on Earth. OK, sometimes I get a map, showing where relatives were from, but nothing to do with race.

You see, Spirit cannot come through and show us how they look now. Just a speck of light or an 'orb' would be a guess, but it would be nothing more than a guess. A Spirit comes through with images and details describing their earthly appearance, otherwise this job would be even harder than it already is. This was a term used by a client to affectionately differentiate between her two grandmas while they were here on Earth. Spirit gave me that piece of evidence to be passed, to identify someone and is in no way an indication that Spirit even considers race after we have passed.

I have been told that this person could be a past life relative but I am still reluctant to fully accept that just yet, only because, with the accounts of reincarnation I have seen, the reincarnations in question, tended to be similar with the past life as far as geographical location, and in one of the cases, a young boy in a Native American community, there was strong evidence to suggest that he was born into the exact same community! Again, without banging on about it, **Surviving Death** on Netflix explains the above story very well.

If you are reading this and have contacted your guide, a guide that happens to be a wise monk, then I feel you are less likely to ridicule what I said, (after all, your guide is a wise monk) and offer me something that my brain can make sense of. Because there's a gap in the understanding here for me and I'm sure many others, that keeps this subject where it is... Questionable!

Incidentally, if it turns out that I'm not crazy and race and colour are just human issues, something that isn't a thing in the Spirit world, that cause so many problems in this world when all we are is an energy once we die, then that is a crying shame that we do this to each other if what follows is totally irrelevant. Don't you think? Is it not healthy to ask a reasonable question to see if someone can give me an answer that makes sense in my head?

I am also the first to admit that I am a bit slow on the uptake occasionally if my stubbornness won't allow me to fully understand. I have given so many readings and given detailed evidence from loved ones, but when I have been asked by a client for a description of a guide, I just get information about the client's current situation. Almost like guides don't describe themselves, because it's not like the client can validate any description I give.

I fully believe we have guides; I just think our guides are more than likely known to us. When I get guide information from the front in my readings, I almost feel like a family member has left the area to my right-hand side and approached the front to take up a role of guidance. Take the stage if you like!

I have family in Spirit around me all the time, and if they do turn out to be my guides but I block them out in search of a preconception or narrative of wisdom that we couldn't possibly get from a guide that isn't a Native American or monk, could it be overcomplicating this? It's just a question I felt was worth raising. My whole understanding with Spirit is that we are all just an energy after and all the same, looking out for our loved ones until we are all together to head on to our next part of the journey.

Believe me; I am so open and will stand corrected if anything in this book that makes no sense to me can be proven or explained in a way that has no holes or openings for more questions. This book isn't all about facts; it's about questioning what doesn't make sense, until it does!

We can take the most well-intentioned lessons that we learn and pass them on with the sole purpose of helping – nothing more, no personal gain, just the will to heal others – and still do damage. Incomplete truths, as explained earlier, for me are more damaging than complete bullshit. The sad truth is that we don't know we are even doing this half the time. As humans, when presented with a view that conflicts with the view of the masses, we have a subconscious dilemma and can totally ignore the rational in favour of the irrational, due to the rational sounding so different from the masses' view.

My point earlier in the book, where I talk about using sage to clear negative Spirits from a space, along with a lot of things I've written, was difficult for me to write. Rationally, to suggest to me that a herb grown in the garden, intended to be used in cooking to make food taste better, is something that can clear an evil Spirit just does not compute in my brain. I cannot understand why this could possibly work, even if there was an evil Spirit!

Because in Spirituality the belief is widely held, I questioned whilst writing about it if I would get a huge backlash. I am fully expecting to, but I have to be honest with my thoughts. In contrast, something that sounded completely stupid to me the first time I heard it was that lemons absorb negative energy. When I first heard this, I thought to myself:

Here we fucking go, another nut job.

Yet after it was explained that it can be used to show the negative energy, not from Spirit, but us; we can make a room feel heavy and negative with our own energy to. Have you ever been in a room after someone has had a big argument in there or got the feeling that you just don't want to be in a room that you walk into?

I had to try it. I brought a bag of lemons, put some in various rooms around my house and just left them there. At the same time, I hid one somewhere in a room belonging to someone who I know is a complete miserable bastard. No names. The lemons at my house are very hard and obviously dried out within the first month, but other than that, no mould, no black spots, just dry lemons. My spy lemon, hidden somewhere I know to be a habitat for a particular grumpy bastard, was different. I had to throw it away about two weeks after I put it there it as it was a mouldy mess, apparently due to being in a negative atmosphere.

2 year old lemons

Something that had originally seemed so silly to me at first, after I had demonstrated it to myself, now didn't seem silly. This takes me back to the fact I will always be learning. I will always be open to things even if they sound silly at first. The key is demonstration. If I can't demonstrate it, I won't waste any time worrying about it, because whether it is wrong or right, I'm wasting energy on hearsay.

It's almost as crazy as spending my whole life in fear of burning in a hell that we have been told to be fearful of, but, unlike mediumship and psychic 'phenomenon' that has countless documented accounts of unexplainable evidence, we are just supposed to go with it and fear it because we are told to, and so many other people do so just go with it.

Has anyone had a near-death experience and come back saying they had seen hell? In fact, after what I said earlier in this book about everything just being light after and fire being a physical thing, it makes even less sense. How does light burn anyway? As I said earlier, if you haven't seen it, treat yourself and watch *Surviving Death* on Netflix, it's a very interesting watch and the near-death experience episode is very good.

I was in the circle I talked about earlier in this book and the topic happened to be Spirit guides; something I had struggled with since day one was the guided Spirit meditations to connect to your guide. My mind just blocked, and I struggled. I enjoy this circle, even though, as you can imagine, I do not hold the same views as everyone. I know I will not always be right so love hearing counter views and it is healthy to keep an open mind and participate.

I put this down to my long-held belief that guides don't need to describe themselves to you because you can't confirm or validate whether it is correct, so why would they try? I always thought descriptions were for loved ones that you can validate. That is, unless the family are the guides, along with Angels.

219

In my readings, like I explained earlier, I get blood relatives to my right and non-blood to my left. I should add that if I feel the hairs stand up on the back of my neck, I know this is the sitter's Angels. If I get a tingling sensation on the top of my head or face, I know this is from the sitter's guides. On reflection, it is rare that I get guides coming forward. As I said earlier in the book, my belief is that Angels are there to get us through the shit times; guides are there when we have our shit together.

Awakenings are currently a common thing. Half the world is waking up and sometimes I almost feel like a fraud saying the same thing over and over when I feel Angels push on my back at the opening of a reading to show that this is an "awakening in progress". The crazy thing about this is, when I read for someone personally, whom I know and who is just asking for a reading the same as they would get their fortune told if they were at the seaside, I don't get that.

I genuinely don't get the Angel push when reading for someone who isn't having a shit time with life at the time of the reading. Repetitive or not, it is the first sign in a reading if Angels are present. Quite often, if Angels are going to come through, the first sensation from Spirit as I open will be from those Angels. That isn't to say we don't all have angels round us, we just get more attention from them when we are having a shit time with life.

To put it as frankly as possible:

My experience tells me that it's ANGELS that are in charge, and if they get a chance to help in any way during a 30-minute reading, then I'm sorry but the other stuff will have to wait; certainly in my readings, because I just go with what comes through as that is what Spirit feels is most important for the client.

For you to be reading a book about awakenings, the chances are you already know that they can be, to be frank, a bit shit and cause very low periods. When you feel that low, you can bet your life that Angels are the ones dragging you through the shit times, giving you signs and trying to give you help and hope.

As silly as it felt saying the word "Angel" at the start of all this, it doesn't anymore because whether you call them Angels, Guardians, or whatever else, they are certainly a part of our lives. They guide too! I know this from experience...

In the circle I was speaking about earlier, like I said, I was struggling with the Spirit guide meditation. I really do struggle in a group setting with confidence. It's due to that fear of being judged I have. We were doing a guided meditation where you must get a message from your Spirit guide and then tell the group how it went.

While I was supposed to be meditating, I was just sitting there thinking the following...

> **Well, I'm going to look like a tit! I'm so worried about looking like a tit I can't even meditate, let alone see this reclusive fucking guide that I need a pissing message from!**

All while totally ignoring all the family in Spirit that, and I hate to say this but certainly on this occasion, I take for granted! I was busy looking for a guide and should have realised they were there all along, but no sooner had I started giving up than I heard this:

"Angels guide too Dad!"

I will explain now that I have a daughter in Spirit who would have been 12 now had she survived the pregnancy, but that was not the case. I often feel her around me and know she is there at the back with my Angels but getting this from her completely floored me emotionally.

After the exercise, we all had to say what Spirit animal, if any, we were aware of and what our guides said. When it came to my turn to talk, I just could not say the words. I struggled so hard to hold it together and it was not going to happen so I said I would just type it in the Zoom chat box instead; then I turned my camera off because that moment for me, was so personal that I just could not share it. Plus, I'm pretty ugly when I'm trying not to get upset.

It is a very difficult thing, knowing I have three children, when being asked how many kids I have to only be able to reply, "Two." This is something I also struggle to go into during readings if I am to be completely honest. When I read for someone, I will often get a number for the amount of children they have. This number, to put it simply, is the number of pregnancies, not necessarily the number of children. This is because Spirit, at first, tells me how many children you have, not necessarily how many children you have who still happen to be in their earthly bodies. I'm not saying this is given to me in every case, but it is common.

A very sad subject but I think it's worth pointing out the above because, to me, it's a beautiful thing. Spirit counts all children because soon after conception, the child is your child, regardless of whether or not they have a human body as well as Spirit energy. It's quite possibly the most important evidence that can be passed and a reminder of the bigger picture. This human life is just a very small part of our journey and, although we may not know exactly what comes next, I can be fairly certain that there is a lot more peace once we take all the earthly Ego stuff out of the mix when passing over. One thing I also can be sure of, is that there is no judgement, just love.

Something I did always think about was the fact that it must be pretty boring for Spirit to be watching over us all the time with nothing else to do, but what we should remember is that time is our thing. Spirits don't measure time and our lives are a just a tiny blip.

Think for one minute of life as being a big game of Tag that you and your loved ones are playing before you have to get back for dinner. The first person in your team to be tagged might wait around for everyone else they were playing with to finish, cheering you on before you are tagged, and you head back. That isn't a whole lot of time out of their life, is it? Yes, this game of tag might be a big ongoing game that has fresh players turning up and joining in, but you won't be waiting around for all of them. You just wait around until the group you know is finished and then you all head back home together. Maybe the last person tagged has someone that they are close to who turned up late in the game, but that is OK; they can still pop back and cheer them on and even be there for them to walk them home when they get tagged.

Maybe Great-Grandad was tagged first and went home with the people he was playing with, popping back every now and then to see how Grandad is getting on in the game, cheering him on until it's clear that he is about to be tagged, so he hangs around to walk home with him, back to the rest of the family.

It sort of explains to me why it is so rare to have Spirit come through for a client if they passed a long time before the client was conceived. Maybe when we have finished watching over those we knew and cared about, we carry on doing the other things in Spirit that we are yet to discover. We may well have ancestors that pop by now and again, but it's our close relatives that I believe are around us the most.

One other thing I think is important to mention in this chapter is imaginary friends... Did you have one? During my readings, be it very occasionally, I have been made aware of a young energy that is around the client but not someone that was a blood relative and not coming through as someone that was known to the client, however they're still there. This is quite rare and the first time I experienced this was for a client who came to me for a completely different reason, certainly not to ask about an imaginary friend that was long in the past ... or so she thought!

She was asking for a reading about a certain subject initially; I asked her later in the reading if she remembered having an imaginary friend as a child, one that was a young boy with light hair. She was completely shocked but said yes. This young boy was very much around her and amazingly showed me a toy RC car that the client explained to me was her favourite toy as a child.

From what this young male in Spirit told me, I was able to tell the client that I was aware of some events that had caused her some emotional issues. You see, imaginary friends that come through in readings are clearly not imaginary. This young boy described the décor of her childhood home perfectly, allowing me to give evidence that allowed her to trust what I was saying

The reason this young boy in Spirit had decided to be around my client was, quite frankly, one of the most heart-warming but at the same time saddest things I have ever experienced whilst doing this.

The young light-haired boy had died due to abuse from his heavy-handed parents. He was trying to protect her and befriended her because he recognised what she was going through. This again shows that we all have this, just that in childhood it's easier to accept because we are children and have no reason to question what we pick up on.

Then, as we get older, we get told we are crazy, or we worry we might look crazy, so we shut it out. What a sad thought it is when you imagine the Spirit around you, there for you, suddenly getting ignored because this world tells us that the Spirit friend you had was just your imagination.

The second time this same client came for a reading she had just lost her dog and it was her imaginary friend who showed me the dog, allowing me to describe it to validate to the client that her imaginary friend was looking after her dog, now in the Spirit world.

The other times I have had imaginary friends come through they have all been describable and confirmed and it's always the same pattern of being around someone experiencing the same type of trauma that they themselves had. It is a part of this work that I find the most fascinating and, although rare, it's always emotional for me.

It makes sense to me also because that imaginary friend, who was quite likely taken due to abuse or neglect, if an only child would have no reason to have to watch over anyone else. I have a very upsetting example also, but it is unfair to talk about it and I am prevented by law from doing so due to a reopened investigation. From what I understand, that is about as far as I can go in the way of details, but it contained enough evidence from this "imaginary" friend to be able to confirm a lot that was previously suspected but unproven.

Whilst on the subject of children and trauma, there is a subject that even I still have trouble getting my head to accept, even though I have witnessed very vivid accounts—past life trauma…

When I was talking about James earlier and said I would talk about his brother's event later in the book, well, this is where I talk about that. This is a good example of thinking I can no longer be shocked and then being genuinely shocked.

You see, there's a big difference in believing in something and actually witnessing something. I have believed in past lives and have no problem believing in them as I have had some fantastic readings myself and carried out many past life regressions, but I won't bore you with that, and instead, talk about Emma, Tom and Evelyn. Tom has a young daughter called Evelyn and both he and his Wife Emma had been wondering why she was having night terrors.

This is something he mentioned one day whilst doing a job for them at my 'day job'. As Tom and James are among some of the few customers at my day job that are aware of my psychic medium work, he asked me if I could see anything that would be causing it, e.g., a Spirit in her room that she may be scared of.

Something he also mentioned was that she seems so concerned all the time; unusually so for a 2-year-old. She tells her parents to call the doctors often and says things that are slightly unusual for someone of that age.

As Tom was talking, I started to pay attention and became aware of one thing I could see. I said I could see an older lady in spirit, leaning over Evelyn in the night, trying to comfort her for some reason. Certainly not the cause of the night terrors, in fact, the complete opposite! (A good example of how spirit could be mistaken for being negative.)

The shocking thing about this is that I could make out the words being said...

"Julie, Rest"

When I said this, every hair on my body stood on end and as with a lot of times drafting this book, the same is happening as I type. My first thought was that I had got it wrong, and Tom said he knows no Julie, so it makes no sense to him. As I started to piece together what was happening, I told him to watch Surviving Death on Netflix before I gave my opinion. This is something that I know, just sounded too crazy for a 'non-spiritualist' (awful term, sorry), without seeing at least a few accounts of unexplainable past life reports. I left the job feeling like Tom now thought I was talking rubbish but to be fair to him, he was open minded and willing to give it the time of day to investigate. From what I was seeing, I could see that this elderly lady in Spirit, was in fact addressing Evelyn as "Julie", strongly suggesting that this was the name of Evelyn in a past life!

This was a completely new one to me. OK, I have carried out a number of past life regressions, but this was a lady in Spirit, addressing one of Evelyn's past lives, a whole different thing entirely! Evelyn was clearly having night terrors because of a trauma in her past life that had carried over with the soul and was manifesting in these night terrors. From what I could see, this older lady in Spirit was there to heal Evelyn and try to remove that Trauma, hence "Julie, Rest"!

Around a week later, he sent me a text asking if it was ok to call as it was quite late. He wanted to tell me about what happened earlier that day with Evelyn. When he called, he told me that both his wife Emma and he had been thinking about what I said this could be and thought they would try something...

While Evelyn was sitting watching TV during the day, playing in the front room, Tom began saying Female Names. Evelyn continued what she was doing and did not respond. You know what's coming...

He listed off various female names to no response and then got to the name 'Julie'... When he did, Evelyn turned round and said "yes?"

Tom and his Wife tried this again a couple of times to make sure it wasn't just a fluke, but the same thing happened. Tom even said the second time, she just stared at him for longer after she had responded. I couldn't help laughing to myself at the thought of how Freaked out Tom must have been, having his daughter staring at him, after answering to a name that was not hers, ignoring all the others!

There is certainly a lot more for me to learn about past lives and certainly would not at this stage, claim to be able to offer past life trauma healing to a 2-year-old. Call me a cynic but I fail to see how I would get any 2-year-old to sit through a past life regression. Sending healing maybe or collaborating with guides could be an option, but apparently things do seem to be getting better for Evelyn, and her night terrors are not as bad. We all have Spirit around us that we can all contact if we wish to. Family, Angels, Guides, Pets, and sometimes even imaginary friends from childhood that weren't so imaginary!

One thing I can be sure of is that it's not Spirit causing trauma and terror. In the case above, it was Spirit trying to sooth and calm, apparently trying to give the healing that was required. The same as any experience I have had with Spirit, and I feel so strongly that we should be free of fear. The biggest reason for that is so we don't miss something that could be a life changing, beautiful experience instead off us panicking and automatically presuming that it's something negative just because we are aware of energy around us.

After recently getting updated by Tom about how it was all going, it seems Evelyn is now very comfortable to talk about the 'purple lady' as she calls her, and has said that she doesn't like cars, along with something else. As I have always said, anything I pass, can only be taken seriously if there is evidence that can be confirmed. In this case, I feel Evelyn answering to the name 'Julie', and now that she is comfortably talking about the 'purple lady' that she talks to, she has revealed that she has heard "Julie shhh" also. It is important to stress here that Evelyn has no idea that I heard the words "Julie, rest", so this was very much a surprise and a fantastic validation.

Evelyn is extremely lucky to have open minded parents that took the time to understand what the issue could be, allowing Evelyn to talk about what is happening without getting told: - "that's silly" or "imaginary friend" and clearly, Evelyn has no fear of the 'purple lady'. She has made it clear she sees her in the day while awake, demonstrating our basic most natural connection to Spirit, with no fear whatsoever! I'm sure many children have been aware of, or had no fear of spirit at that age. It would be quite normal for us to just say "That's silly", blame something medical for the terrors, get a prescription, and cover an issue up, leaving the child having to re-learn what they think they know, to prepare them for all the ghost stories, horror films, and human stories of evil that will put the fear with the unhealed trauma, thanks to humans passing fear.

What if we thought about what damage could be happening in some situations? And where we could be doing damage if we do dismiss everything without considering other possibilities? We only have textbooks and what science tells us is fact, but I can only be honest with what I say... I think that dismissing something a child says, by saying it is silly or imaginary, could cause emotional issues moving forward in life, subconsciously damaging confidence.

What if something, that was simply a fact to them, was dismissed or ridiculed? Is their mind now programmed to accept that their reality is not always correct? Could that now make it easy to be manipulated in future relationships, now your subconscious mind is taught it can't always trust its reality?

How? Because a child that tells you they talk to someone that you cannot see, may well be talking to Spirit. Spirit may be doing what they can for that child to heal the soul that may be damaged from a past life or even because of a current life trauma. Now if that is actually the case, only for you to say it is not happening, whether intentionally or not...

That is Gaslighting!

If you had a pet dog in the house, and a child talked about that dog, only to be told that the dog does not exist, over and over again, what damage could that do to the child emotionally? Denying what is clearly a fact to the child. Because IF that child is talking about a Spirit that they are very well in tune with and is very much there, then it is no different than saying the dog is imaginary!

Gaslighting is a colloquialism, loosely defined as making someone question their own reality. The term may also be used to describe a person who

presents a false narrative to another group or person which leads them to doubt their perceptions and become misled, disoriented, or distressed.

Source: Wikipedia

Maybe if this was all looked at with more of an open mind, even just considered a possibility, then we might have less mental health issues in the world as a result. I say that because I am in no doubt whatsoever that Evelyn, a child I have never met, is seeing the lady she is talking about, and is in no way an 'imaginary' friend. The reality is, that Evelyn has a lady in Spirit looking out for her and obviously, that is Evelyn's fact. If she was told that her fact, was not fact, it would certainly be gaslighting and we know how emotionally damaging it is to take someone's reality and tell them it is not reality. Evelyn is very lucky to have the parents she does.

The facts we have, from the above, are that enough evidence was presented to reasonably assume that Evelyn had carried with her, trauma from a past life. This, to me is something that opens up a world of questions relating to how we approach conditions such as PTSD. How do we treat something that could have been caused by an event in a different lifetime? Especially if the root of any condition is buried deep in the subconscious?

We have only scratched the surface of trauma and resulting emotional problems as a race, and as we look back through history, "facts" that we learn, have changed with time and new discoveries. Maybe all this will too one day. I 100% believe that eventually, the trauma we carry over with our souls into this life, will be taken seriously enough to garner research into how we can treat it.

I am not here to tell you how to get through this or what to believe, only to tell you how I got through it in the hope you can pick up some tips that might help. If you did pick up a few things along the way that will help you, great; once you have the basics sussed and become comfortable with how you are dealing with it all without fear or anxiety you have pretty much nailed it. No one owns Spirituality and no one has any more of a right to explore it than you do. Your greatest teachers are around you in Spirit so if you can tune in, you will know you are on track with all the guidance you need.

I do not believe in instructions when it comes to awakenings unless it is to show to you how Spirits pass messages. One of the most important points in this whole book is that once you have that trust and are comfortably receiving messages from Angels, Guides, Family, or whatever other Spirit we can name, you have all the guidance you need, from the experts!

Some of us have an awakening and pass messages. Some of us have an awakening and become great energy healers. Some of us have an awakening and see the world clearer while carrying on with our lives but now with that little bit of comfort that was not there before. No way is a wrong way so we cannot let anyone tell us what we have to do or how we *have* to do it unless we specifically ask for direction.

I can see us slowly becoming increasingly aware of consciousness and what it means for us, and this is something I honestly feel is now facing a new turning point of acceptance.

This acceptance will hopefully do wonderful things for us as a race if we do not destroy ourselves first or try to monetise it, or own it like a piece of technology, because that is not how we will see any improvement. The improvement will come when we stop with the control, fear, hate, and everything else that we seem consumed with during our time here on Earth. Our time here is just a blip in our existence, but the learning we get from it can shape our souls for the future and what is yet to come when we pass over. If we can take anything that we do learn from Spirit, the most important thing, the number one priority, is that we need to learn to accept each other without judgement, without control, and, most importantly, without fear.

Going from being a complete sceptic, to KNOWING what I know now, the whole world and the way we look at life is slowly changing for the better. Through the ages, we have killed each other for such stupid reasons, destroying the planet at the same time with our drive for more – more convenience, more money, more power, more choice – and now we really are at the point as a race where something must give, and Spirit knows this.

The hardest thing for me to understand is the reason why we cause so much pain to each other, because none of it matters after, in Spirit. What does matter after, is the consciousness we have and what we did for our souls while we were here. Soul lessons don't have to be doom and gloom either.

Arguably, something more important than that is if we have been gifted a life to live and experience, have we made the most of it and enjoyed it enough? If you haven't so far, change something. If we can't enjoy this experience fully, and appreciate exactly how short this experience is, then we are not doing it right.

Maybe the experience is just a test or a game, but the fact we do have is that there is nothing after but love and the lessons we have learned. All the other shit we are consumed with stays here and all we have to do is decide whether we want to leave with an enriched soul or let the shit that distracts us consume our souls.

What if the technology we try so hard to make better and better was already perfect around the time we built so many amazing buildings, hundreds, even thousands, of years ago in perfect alignment all around the world? Before any explorers had even set sail, but with the same building methods. Could we even begin to think about how we could do that today without traveling and without any form of communication other than our minds?

We have seen so many ages throughout history that have seen us advance as a race. There was one thing with this advancement that we were losing though...

Through the Stone Age, Bronze, and Iron Ages, we had something far more advanced than we did today. In our recent sub ages, e.g., Industrial age, Space age, and Information age, we have seen rapid advancements in technology, improving at a rate that will see things become easier for us, almost by the day.

We have phones with screens that enable us to have a face-to-face meeting with someone on the other side of the world, wireless internet beamed down from space, gps technology that can take you to any destination you desire, and tourist trips to space. The advances in technology are amazing, but there may be one problem with these advancements; the resources that are becoming more and more scarce. We are now getting to a point of near self-destruction because of our need for more and more. We are using up the earths resources at an alarming rate, filling space with satellites and even using our fantastic minds to build weapons that can destroy the whole planet in a matter of hours. Where does that leave the world?

Our developments in communication technology remain some way off catching up with technology we already are in possession of. Hundreds of years ago we communicated in a more highly sophisticated way than we currently do with our internet, screens, and satellites. Spirit sees what is happening and it could be the reason why so many in the world are waking up. Before the modern ages and the noise of today's life we communicated like many animals do today, telepathically, and arguably with the help of Spirit. The technology was free, and the only resource needed was a clear head. Something we get less of today, maybe due to the technology we are creating to catch up with a communication system we already have.

We have so much about us that is not tapped into, but this is only the start. Once we quieten the noise and focus on listening to our higher consciousness with all the noise of this modern, stressful, life stripped away, something amazing will happen. We will open ourselves up to the best, most high-tech communication system imaginable. We will also loose the tie we have to things that are the focus of so many in this life. This short blip we call life, is such a small part of our journey. Our existence is so much more than these earthly bodies, and the short life we know now is just a brief experience for us in something so much bigger.

We are edging closer to a new age for humanity that some are already aware of. An age that will help humans survive moving forward, and even though we may not be here to see the positive changes that will come with this age while we are in our earthly bodies, we will certainly have a lot of time in Spirit afterwards to see what our experiences now, were the beginning of.

This is the age you are at the forefront of, and you have an amazing head start...

SEAN GRAHAM

Ladies and Gentlemen,

Welcome to the Age of the Awakening...